Group Games
Relaxation & Concentration

CMHA
Pictou County
Branch
902-755-9441

This material has been placed by
The Canadian Mental Health Association
Pictou County Branch.

Made possible by a grant from the
Nova Scotia Gaming Foundation

D0143788

Group Games
Relaxation & Concentration

ROSEMARIE PORTMANN
& ELISABETH SCHNEIDER

Speechmark

Speechmark Publishing Ltd
Telford Road · Bicester · Oxon OX26 4LQ · United Kingdom

Originally published in German by Don Bosco Verlag München under the title *Spiele zur Entspannung und Konzentration*, © Don Bosco Verlag, München 1998

Published in 2002 by
Speechmark Publishing Ltd, Telford Road, Bicester, Oxon OX26 4LQ, UK
www.speechmark.net

002-5109/Printed in the United Kingdom/1030

British Library Cataloguing in Publication Data

Portmann, Rosemarie
    Relaxation & concentration. – (Group Games)
    1. Attention in children   2. Relaxation   3. Group games
    I. Title   II. Schneider, Elisabeth
    155.4'13'1532

ISBN 0 86388 419 9

Contents

About the Authors

Rosemarie Portmann Dip (Psychol) is the manager of the educational psychology service for the local education authority in Wiesbaden, Germany. She is also an adviser to the Parents Association in Hessen.

Rosemarie is a lecturer at the Institute for Educational Pedagogy and Teaching Methods in the Elementary and Primary Department of the University of Frankfurt.

She is the author of several successful games books and other specialist publications, including *Relaxation & Concentration* and *Dealing with Aggression*, both in the 'Group Games' series, which are also published by Speechmark.

Elisabeth Schneider is the pedagogical head of a comprehensive school in Giessen.

Acknowledgements

Thank you to Lilo Seelos, the translator.

Note: The text sometimes refers to the leader or the child as 'he', for the sake of clarity alone.

Games

Introduction

Hectic pace, tension and the inability to collect oneself and get some peace are signs of our times. Verbal and physical restlessness, distractibility and a lack of concentration are among the most common difficulties that our children experience at school, at home and in their free time. Finding a balance between work and relaxation is also difficult for adolescents and adults, regardless of their age. The opportunity for reflection and leisure has become rare in an age where dynamism and constant activity are said to guarantee success.

However resolving tensions through calmness and relaxation are essential in order to maintain mental and physical health. It is important to explore and develop one's own strengths and, thus strengthened, to be able to consciously focus, concentrate and do what is really important.

The exercises and games collected in this book can be effective aids for re-establishing relaxation and quietness; for creating new receptiveness, and for practising attention and concentration with all the senses and the whole body. They strengthen awareness of one's own abilities, and trust in others. Additionally, they facilitate fantasy and creativity. Harmony and social cohesion in any group – whether of children, teenagers, young or old adults – are improved through joint experiences and joint fun in play.

Of course, severe concentration difficulties and states of restlessness cannot be cured by such exercises and games alone; they require expert advice and, at times, specialist therapy.

HOW TO USE THE GAMES

There are many more exercises and games for relaxation and concentration than those that have been collected in this book. Games included in this collection were selected with the following criteria in mind:

◆ All exercises and games can be carried out with groups of 20–25 participants, so that everybody has something to do and no one becomes bored. However, some exercises would be more successful with fewer players, or with a division into sub-groups, and this will specifically be pointed out.

◆ Everybody, regardless of their age, can participate. All exercises and games have been tried with children from the age of six or seven, adolescents and adults. Sometimes, the basic game may need to be varied according to the age of group members. In this case, the game description will contain pointers as to how to play in a way that will be successful and enjoyable for a particular age group.

◆ The games can be used in learning as well as leisure environments. They are suitable – unless stated otherwise – for short as well as longer interruptions and resolutions of restless or tense group situations, and for the creation of special autonomous play times.

Little or no preparation, no special materials, and no special room are needed to carry out any of the exercises and games. Generally, it will be enough to move tables to one side and create a seated circle – and even that is not always required. Weather permitting, a number of the exercises can be played outside. Materials that are sometimes required are usually available in a group room, or easily obtainable: paper, pencils, scissors, chalk, a scarf or blindfold which, rolled up, can also function as a ball; common objects, such as spoons, erasers, coins, and so on. Should a particular item not be available, it can easily be replaced by another. One element of preparation, however, is indispensable: the leader – or one of the group members – should have played the game themselves once before introducing it to the group. No game can facilitate quietness, relaxation and concentration if the leader is busily trying to remember how it works.

It is difficult to say exactly how much time is needed for each individual game. Often, the time a game takes will depend on whether the group already knows it or has to learn it first. Playing time also depends on the age and number of players; the game variation chosen and, of course, the number of rounds played. Many of the games do not have a 'natural' end: they can be repeated as long as players feel like continuing. There are exercises that can be fitted in quickly among 'normal' group activities to calm, to relax, and to re-establish an ability to work. Others require considerably more time and leisure. Every group leader has to find the optimal play time for each new group. This will also depend on their own experiences of a particular game.

None of the game rules are written in stone. No limits are set to the fantasy and creativity of the group. Depending on age, number of participants, and needs of the group members, as well as the physical and time constraints, a game or exercise can be made easier or more difficult, or changed in some other way. Most games come with a number of variations; however, that does not mean that these are the only ones possible. The only important thing is that the rules of each game are agreed on jointly and unambiguously prior to each new round – otherwise it is unlikely that the group members will settle down and concentrate.

All games are designed in such a way that they do not need to have winners and losers – they are designed to bring relaxation, concentration, fun and enjoyment for all group members. Individual players may have to sit out some games for one or two rounds. However, although not 'active', they often still have a special function in the course of the game. Where this is the case, it is pointed out in the individual instructions. Games that also lend themselves to competition contain respective pointers.

Care has been taken to ensure that all exercises and games are easy to learn and carry out; they do not require the leader to have special 'therapeutic' abilities. Even the simple quietness and relaxation exercises can be carried out by any leader with any group, presupposing participants know each other reasonably well, and enjoy playing together. Nevertheless, it is possible that individual members may not wish to participate in a particular exercise. Such wishes should be respected in every case. No one, even young children, should be pressurised into participating in self-reflective exercises that they do not want to participate in. Such group members should simply be asked to keep quiet so that they do not disturb the others. After every quietness, meditation and awareness exercise, group members should be given the time and opportunity to talk about their experiences during the exercise – with a number of particularly familiar group members, or with the whole group. Some games are accompanied by a particular tune. Special musical skills are not required. Tunes can easily be read or played from a sheet, and are likely to be known already by some of the group members.

All games and exercises in this collection have a common purpose: they are meant to facilitate relaxation and concentration. However, this will not be possible if, under the instruction of a nervous group leader, a group is trying too hard: calmness and attention cannot be forced. The exercises and games recommended here will only fulfil their purpose if the group leader is balanced and calm, and the group members are experiencing themselves and the situation as unsettled and are developing a need for calmness. If this also results in enjoyment of the activities, trust in one's own abilities, and fun in the proposed games, it is unlikely that anything will go wrong. Incidentally, it is not just quietness and calmness in a group that indicate that a game is fulfilling its purpose of creating relaxation and concentration; laughing, having fun together, and feeling happy are also clear signs that the games are working.

To provide a better overall view, exercises and games are divided into four main groups which take into consideration contents, purpose and possibilities. However, a totally unambiguous categorisation is not possible: many of the games, and particularly their numerous variations, could belong to more than one group. As a result, the groupings made here are subjective. They are based on our experiences of using the games in leisure and school groups with children and teenagers, as well as with adult further education groups. The main groups are as follows.

Games for Reducing Restlessness & Agitation

Many people – young and old – find themselves in a continuous state of agitation and tension. They cannot bear to sit still, to not talk, to not do anything. The more stillness is demanded of them, the more they try to force themselves to be still, the more restless they become. Busy activity and presence of others further increases their state of excitation. Initially, such people have to be given the possibility within the group to act out their restlessness and excitation without fully losing control of themselves. At the same time, inhibited group members, too, have to be given an incentive for articulation and movement, as well as instruction as to how to carry these out.

Calming & Awareness Games/Kim's Games

Inner calm is more than simply being still and keeping one's mouth closed. It means turning to one's own inner centre, to listen to oneself and to gather inner strengths, in order to gain trust in oneself and others. A prerequisite for this is to experience one's own body and to admit one's own emotions and feelings, to sharpen all senses, and to be consciously aware of one's own person and the environment.

A sub-group of such awareness exercises are the so-called 'Kim's Games', which take their name from the eponymous character in one of Rudyard Kipling's novels. The orphan Kim learns, with the help of jewels, to increase his observation and memory skills to the highest degree. Kim's Games demand and practise concentrated awareness and differentiation. There are Kim's Games for all senses, not just for looking, but also for hearing, touching, smelling and tasting and, of course, for concentration on existing knowledge.

Attention & Thinking Games

Many games require luck and fantasy. The exercises and games that have been put together here, however, cannot succeed without conscious attention and willing concentration: tasks can only be solved through exact observation and precise thinking and problem-solving. To manage them, players must, above all, use their minds.

Concentration Games for the Whole Body

Concentration is not just a thing of the mind. There are also exercises and games that involve the whole body. To do these, one has not only to strain one's head, but also to concentrate on one's body, on facial expression, gesture and movements, with or without the support of music and text. Movement and expression games are an ideal way of combining the reduction of restlessness with the building of concentration, facilitating a sense of well-being within the group, and they are also good fun.

PUBLISHER'S NOTE

The original version of this text used German songs in some of the activities. Rather than substitute these with English-language songs, the publisher felt that it would be better if users of this book substituted them with English or American songs, or songs that are relevant to the culture of the children within the group. Alternatively, as the music is also published here, the group leader/teacher could teach the songs in this book and use them in their activities.

Games for
Reducing
Restlessness
& Agitation

1 Employee

Players are usually standing or seated in a circle, but they may also remain seated as they are – for example at tables in a group room or classroom. One member takes on the role of leader and names actions that the other members have to carry out in mime.

For example, the leader begins with 'Jump' – everybody jumps. Then he says 'Cough' – everybody coughs. 'Pretend to chop wood' follows – everybody makes an appropriate movement, and so on. It is important to begin with activities that require a lot of movement and, if possible, keep the whole body busy. Gradually, the actions should become calmer, and end something like this: 'Shake your arms'; 'Shake your legs'; 'Sit down'; 'Yawn'; 'Support your head with your arms' or 'Put your head on the table'; 'Close your eyes'; 'Breathe calmly and evenly'; 'Pretend to sleep …'

After about a minute the leader says, 'Wake up'; 'Remain sitting quietly' – and everybody wakes up and sits quietly. The game is finished.

This exercise is particularly useful to reduce physical restlessness in children and teenager groups, but it also helps adults to dampen down nervousness and restlessness.

2   Poor Black Pussy Cat

All players are seated in a circle. One of them is the black pussy cat and crawls around the middle of the circle on all fours. Eventually, it stops on its knees in front of any player it chooses, and tries to attract their attention by making cat-like grimaces and movements, or trying silky purring and pathetic meowing. The player the pussy cat has stopped in front of has to stroke it and say three times in a row, 'Poor black pussy cat', in a sympathetic tone of voice. However, they are not allowed to say anything else to the pussy cat, or to laugh or get worked up in any other way. If they lose their calm, they have to take the place of the poor black pussy cat in the middle of the circle.

If the pussy cat is unable to get that player to lose their calm, it has to find a new victim.

After the number of attempts agreed prior to starting the game – perhaps three or four – either a new pussy cat is chosen, or the game ends, because quite obviously it has achieved its purpose: to create calmness and self-control.

3 Blinking

This game requires an uneven number of players to stand in pairs, one behind the other, in a circle. The player who is left over now tries to tempt the 'front person' of one of the pairs to come over to them by blinking. The partner of the person who has been blinked at has to try to hold them. If they manage to escape, nevertheless, the 'back person' who has been left behind becomes the new blinker. A person who has been blinked at and who manages to get away goes and stands behind their new partner, so that, in the course of the game, every player gets an opportunity to be blinked at, or experiences having to hold. During the game, the 'front people' can also sit on chairs with their partners standing behind them. One chair must, of course, remain free.

This game can also be played with an even number of players. In this case, all players are seated in a circle that has one more chair than there are players. The person who has the empty chair next to them on their left now invites any player to change into the empty chair by blinking at them. The respective right neighbour is responsible for looking after their left neighbour, and has to try to hold them back. Of course, the neighbour is only allowed to raise their hands when they notice that their neighbour is indeed being blinked at.

Blinking is a very fast game, where the players who are on the move at any one time change quickly. Therefore it is particularly suitable to provide a short break during tense activities, addressing increasing restlessness and providing some relaxation, for example, during long discussions, group work or lessons.

④ Musical Chairs

All the chairs – one chair fewer than there are players – are positioned in a row in such a way that seats and backs of the chairs alternate. The leader now starts a musical tape or begins to sing, whistle, play an instrument, or tell a story. During this, the other players are walking around the row of chairs.

All of a sudden, the leader abruptly stops the music or story: now, all players have to find a chair to sit on as quickly as possible. The player who is left over drops out. One chair is then removed and the game starts again, until only one chair and one player are left.

For this game, the group should not be too big, otherwise it will take a long time for the row of chairs to be reduced to one; the players who have already dropped out start getting bored, and the intended effect of dampening restlessness may have the opposite outcome.

5   Don't Turn Around, There's Someone Creeping About

All players, except one, stand or sit in a circle facing the middle. The remaining player is given a scarf in which a knot has been made, and has to walk around the outside of the circle. During this, the group sings: 'Don't turn around, there's a creep about. If you turn around or laugh you will get told off.' This song is repeated continuously. At some point, the player drops the scarf as inconspicuously as possible behind another player in the circle. That player has to pick it up and try to catch up with the 'creep'. The player who first gets to the empty place is allowed to sit down; the other becomes the 'creep' for the next round.

This game is well known internationally and is, therefore, particularly suitable for groups with (small or big numbers of) foreign group members.

(6) Railway

The group members remain sitting where they are. One player is declared the 'locomotive'. With appropriate sound effects, this person moves slowly through the group and puts together his 'train' by asking players, one after the other, to join the back of the train as 'wagons'. They form the train by putting both hands on the shoulders of the person in front of them. They add their own sound effects. Once all group members have joined in, the train continues to do a few laps until the 'locomotive', or the group leader, calls out 'Attention please! This train is now approaching the main station', so that players have to prepare themselves for the imminent end of the game, and slow down their pace. When they hear the words, 'The train stops', all players have to stop all train noises, stand quietly, and then return silently to their original places.

However, the game can also be played so that the individual wagons are disconnected from the train one after the other and, with appropriate words, are escorted back to their place: for example, 'Through-coach John stays in this station', 'Through-coach Hannah will be disconnected here', and so on. Smaller children, for whom this game is particularly well suited, find it easier to maintain the calming state that has been created by the game when they are addressed personally.

7 Family Search

Before the game starts, one player has to prepare 'family cards' – at least as many cards as there are players. The group will get the most fun out of this game if the family names all sound similar – for example, Harris, Paris, Narris, Farris, Barris, and so on.

Every family has the same number of cards – for example father, mother, child and dog:

Harris father	Harris mother	Harris child	Harris dog

Name-cards are then shuffled and put in a box or bag from which each player has to draw one card. At the command of the game leader, everybody starts looking for 'their' family members by loudly calling their family name. Every completed family then sits as follows: the father takes his place on a chair; the mother sits on the father's lap; the child on the mother's lap, and the dog lies at everyone's feet. If there are further family members, a place to sit is agreed for them prior to starting the game.

When everybody has finished their family search, the 'dogs' are allowed to do a lap of honour through the room and bark to their heart's content, before they finally settle at the feet of their masters.

This game is particularly well suited to calming down groups of children, but is also enjoyed by teenagers and adults. However, while the families are looking for each other, it will continue to be somewhat noisy!

8 Walking Like an Old Man

A leader beats a drum or plays music from a tape. At the same time, they give instructions to the other players as to how they should move freely around the room to the rhythm of the music; for example, like

◆ An old man
◆ A rambler carrying a heavy rucksack
◆ A father pushing a push chair
◆ A young woman who feels really happy
◆ A child walking across rocks with bare feet
◆ A woman with her boyfriend under an umbrella
◆ A young man who is carrying a ladder with someone else
◆ A super sportsman, who is playing table tennis with a beginner, and so on.

A variation of this exercise can involve paired work, with or without 'real' equipment. For example, two players can

◆ throw a ball or bean bag from one to the other
◆ dance with each other
◆ chase each other
◆ carry a chair together, and so on.

Playing a rhythmical instrument during the game facilitates the mime, especially for players who are out of practice or self-conscious about their movements. However, movement mimes can also work without musical accompaniment and without any special preparation: restlessness and tension are eased noticeably.

(9) Thunderstorm

First of all, the group as a whole thinks about what characterises a thunderstorm and how this could be portrayed: for example, distant rumbles of thunder could be represented by shuffling feet; individual claps of thunder by stamping feet; rain by drumming fingers on tables; wind by howling noises; sheet lightning by little sharp screams; lightning by a loud, shrill scream, and so on.

The individual elements of a thunderstorm are then shared out among the players. One player is chosen as a leader, who triggers the thunderstorm and determines its course. For example, moving closer from a distance, it becomes heavier and heavier, until it gradually becomes quieter as it fades away into the distance again.

Such a thunderstorm can have a cleansing effect. Once it has been introduced, it can be used to get a group to relax quickly in between tasks, when they have worked hard, or when they are very excited.

(10) Ball-Bearing

All players except one sit on chairs not too close together in a circle. One seat is empty. The remaining player stands in the middle of the circle and tries to sit down on the empty chair. The others try to prevent them doing so, by quickly moving from one chair to the next, and back. If the player in the middle finally manages to sit down despite this, the player who is now left over has to go into the middle, and themselves try to sit down again.

Players will be able to focus better on the task if talking is not allowed during the game.

11 Puppets

Players form pairs. One partner of each pair lies down on the floor, or sits down on a chair. That partner turns into a puppet and is not allowed to move unaided. The other partner becomes the puppeteer and 'pulls all the strings' in mime, at the head, shoulders, elbows, hands, knees, feet, and so on. The puppet is made to stand up, to walk, or to make any other – wooden – movements.

Of course, several or all puppeteers can get together and use their puppets to create a statue, a scene, and so on.

After a period of time agreed before the game starts, roles are swapped around, so that every player can have a turn at being puppet and puppeteer.

The puppet play can also be accompanied and guided by music.

12 Human Machine

The players use their bodies to build a 'machine' that moves and makes noises. In order to do this, every player has to touch at least one other player and represent a machine part by, for example, wobbling with their head and making a hissing noise; twitching with the little finger of their left hand and making a bleeping noise or stamping with their right foot and making a humming noise, and so on.

This game works particularly well after group members have been sitting for a long time.

13 Dead Quiet

The group (the mice) are seated in a circle, on the floor or on chairs, quiet as mice and very still. In the middle of the circle is a blanket or a large newspaper. One player creeps around the middle like a cat. If one of the mice moves or makes a sound, the cat touches them with its 'paws' and takes them into the middle as its catch.

After a little while, the cat feels tired. It pulls the blanket or newspaper over its head and has a rest. Now all the mice, including the ones that have been caught, are allowed to move. They can walk around, make a racket, and even tease the cat. However, they have to be careful: as soon as the cat throws off the blanket or newspaper everybody has to return to their seats in the circle as quietly and as quickly as possible, including the mice that had previously been caught. However, this time the first mouse to be caught by the cat has to change roles with it.

The game becomes easier for the cat if, during the rest period, a chair is removed from the circle, so that one mouse is left over.

If this game is played with a group of children, it is even more fun when the mice do not sit on their chairs, but have to crawl underneath them.

The alternation of tension and free movement helps groups to become able to work and concentrate again.

14 Neighbours

All except one player are seated in a circle. There is no chair for the left-over player. Therefore, they have to walk around the circle and ask any player: 'Who would you like to have as your neighbours?' The player who is being addressed now has to name two fellow players who then have to quickly change places with their original neighbours. During this exchange of seats, the player who is standing has to try to grab one of the vacated chairs. Whoever does not get a chair has to stay in the middle, and the game starts anew.

15) Swapping Numbers

For this game, number cards are needed – at least as many as there are players. All players have to know which numbers are used in the game. The cards are shuffled and, before the game begins, everybody draws from a box or bag a number, which they have to keep strictly secret.

Now all players, except one, sit in a circle. The remaining player stands in the middle of the circle and calls any two numbers. The two players who have drawn those numbers have to change seats and, during this exchange, the player in the middle has to try to get one of the places. The player who is now left without a seat becomes the next number-caller.

As the game progresses, those players who pay attention and have a good memory have the advantage. Gradually, they will remember which player had which number, and can thus be strategically clever when calling numbers.

16 Fruit Basket

All players are seated in a circle, and divide themselves into a number of types of fruit: for example, cherries, apples, plums, pears, bananas, and so on. Now one player is chosen to lead the first round. He goes into the middle of the circle, and his chair is moved to the side.

The leader calls out two types of fruit: for example, 'apples' and 'pears'. The players who belong to these types of fruit have to change seats. The leader also tries to find a place for himself. The player who is left in the end now goes into the middle and calls out two types of fruit that have to change this time. If he calls 'fruit basket', all players have to change seats.

Instead of types of fruit from the fruit basket, other objects or living things, such as zoo animals, tools from a tool box, coins from a purse, flowers from the garden, and so on, can also be used.

17) Ox at the Mountain

One of the players – the 'ox' – faces the wall – the 'mountain'. Behind their back, against the opposite wall of the room, the other players are lined up next to each other. The player facing the wall now calls, 'Ox at the mountain'. As long as the player is calling, the other players are allowed to move towards the ox. They have to be careful as they do so: as soon as the 'ox' has finished calling, they turn around. Those players who are surprised in mid-movement have to return to the start line. The player who first makes it to the mountain without being noticed by the 'ox' becomes the new 'ox at the mountain'.

This game is played mainly outdoors, but is also suitable for reducing physical restlessness in a room if the group is not too big. One simply has to try it first.

18　Orchestra Rehearsal

Every player produces a sound that is clearly different from those produced by the others. When everybody has found 'their' sound, they begin, on the leader's signal, to quietly produce it.

In the course of the game, the leader can change the volume and tempo of all the 'instruments', or even individual 'musicians', or groups of musicians, through previously agreed commands. For example, raised arms means 'louder', lowered arms means 'quieter'. If the leader waves his raised arms, this means 'louder and faster'; if he makes a calming movement with both arms, this means 'slower and quieter', and so on. If he spreads out both arms and keep them still, this means 'pause', and all instruments have to stop suddenly.

Once the group is familiar with the game, it can be used for a quick calming break, especially when there is a lot of verbal restlessness or general chatter.

19 Horse Racing

All players, including the leader, are seated in a circle. They imitate the noises and atmosphere of horse racing. This begins with all players tapping their thighs and saying: 't-rot, t-rot, t-rot …' This movement and mumbling is maintained throughout the game. In addition, the leader indicates what else to do by calling out and demonstrating:

◆ 'Right-hand bend' – everybody leans to the right;
◆ 'Left-hand bend' – everybody leans to the left;
◆ 'Jump' – everybody hints at a jumping movement by briefly raising their arms and getting up;
◆ 'Double-jump' – everybody hints at the same jumping movement twice;
◆ 'Treble-jump' – everybody hints at the same jumping movement three times;
◆ 'Spectator stands' – everybody cheers;
◆ 'Pile up among the horses' – everybody boos;
◆ 'Water ditch' – everybody uses their fingers on their lips to make a bubbling sound;
◆ 'Lost a horse shoe' – everybody makes 'plop' sound by putting their fingers in their cheeks, and so on.

The list can be extended by many more noises or movements.

The 'horse race' is particularly suitable for reducing verbal and physical restlessness and, in addition, is much enjoyed by all age groups.

20) Rat-Catcher

One player turns into a rat-catcher. Every other player touched by the rat-catcher has to follow them. And this is how it works. All players remain in their seats or move around freely in the room. The rat-catcher walks up to one of them and touches them somewhere on the body – for example, the back of the head. The player concerned now has to touch the back of their head with their right hand (left-handed players are allowed to use their left hand), and quietly follow the rat-catcher. The rat-catcher approaches another player and touches them – for example, on the left shoulder. With their hand on their left shoulder, this player must now follow the rat-catcher, too, and so on, until all players are walking behind the rat-catcher, each with their hand on the place where they have been touched by the rat-catcher.

Eventually, the rat-catcher speaks the magic word everybody is waiting for, 'Simsalabim', and all players take a deep intake of breath. They are free again and quietly return to their places.

If the game is played with small children, who find the general quietness after being freed together difficult, they can be freed individually by name and sent back to their place. In that case, the group should not be too big.

21 Rhythm Avalanche

A leader begins to clap a rhythm. When he gives a sign, all other players join in the rhythm. The game can be made more difficult by asking only one player to join in at a time, until, in the end, everybody is clapping. Even more concentration is required during this exercise when the next player is not chosen through a previously agreed sequence, but by the leader making eye contact. The exercise can finish as it started: one by one, players stop clapping, again on the leader's signal, until, in the end, only the leader is left clapping.

The game can also be changed so that the leader varies the rhythm and volume during clapping, either for everybody or for individual groups.

Advanced players can also carry out this exercise without any sound, using mimed clapping only.

22 Giant and Dwarf

The leader tells the story of the giant and the dwarf, and accompanies it with corresponding gestures that have to be copied by all players. For example, the story may go as follows:

The giant (arms and body are stretched up high) and the dwarf (squatting down, arms by the side of the body) live together in a beautiful house. In the morning, the giant (arms and body are stretched up high) wakes up first and gets out of bed (taking a big step with knees up high and arms stretched out). Then he opens the window (corresponding movement with stretched arms), and has a good stretch (stretching the whole body with arms up high). Now the dwarf also jumps out of bed (squatting down, arms by the side and jumping). He walks up to the giant (squatting down, arms by the side and taking a few steps), and they take it in turns to have a good stretch (standing up, lengthening and stretching is alternated with squatting down and arms by the side several times). The giant now takes two steps towards his clothes (taking two big steps with a straight body and arms up high), and the dwarf takes four small steps to his clothes (squatting down, arms angled at the side and taking four little steps). Both get dressed, then the giant takes three big steps (taking three big steps stretched up), and the dwarf takes six little steps (six jumps in a squatting position with arms by the side) towards the door and – suddenly both of them disappear.

The story can be changed as you like: it can become shorter or longer; other characters with corresponding movements can be added, and so on. It can even be a totally different story, depending on the age and needs of the group. The only important thing is that the story is accompanied by movements that facilitate alternating movements of tension and relaxation.

(23) **Key Runner**

All players except one stand or sit in a circle. The one player walks around in a circle with a bunch of keys. After a while, he offers his hand to another player and the two walk around together in a circle. Then the second player picks another player from the circle, and so on, until a longish line has formed. At some point, the first player suddenly drops the bunch of keys. Everybody now has to try to get a place in the circle again. The player who is left over, or is the last to move around, gets the bunch of keys and the game starts anew.

(24) Animal Hunt

Prior to the start of play, the leader has to prepare pieces of paper with animal names, with each animal featuring twice. Then every player is given one of the pieces of paper. Listening to music or the command of the leader, all players walk around the room, continuously exchanging their pieces of paper. When the music stops suddenly, or the leader gives the agreed signal, everybody looks at their piece of paper and reads what animal they happen to be right now. By imitating the respective animal noise, they try to find the second animal of their kind.

This game is suitable for reducing verbal and physical restlessness – not only in children.

25 Tomato Salad

The group is seated in a circle. One member is chosen as the leader. A couple of players are sent outside the door. The remaining players think about a multisyllabic word or two-word combination, for example 'to-ma-to sa-lad' and the leader divides the group into as many sub-groups as there are syllables. The individual syllables are assigned to the sub-groups. The players outside the door are called in. At the leader's signal, all players in the circle say or call out their syllable at the same time. The 'guessers' have to try to make out the syllables, put them together and determine the word. To do that, they are allowed to walk around the circle and discuss among themselves.

Guessing becomes more difficult when only one player is sent out and has to find the solution on their own. Instead of multisyllabic words, you can also share out and even sing beginnings of songs that are known to everybody, for example, 'If you're happy and you know it …'.

Caution: the game generates noise and is not suitable for rooms that are poorly soundproofed. However, it is useful for calming down groups that have become restless, as well as those that are unable to listen any more.

26 Fossilising

Players move around the room freely. One turns into a magician, who can 'fossilise' everybody else by touching them; that is, a player who has been touched has to 'freeze' in mid-movement. They can be saved if a player who is still free to walk about touches them.

The game becomes more difficult when talking and calling is not allowed. Fossilised players can then only use mime to attract the attention of free players to themselves, and ask them without words to save them. They have to control not only their desire to move, but also their wish to talk or scream.

Calming &
Awareness Games

(27) Sound of Silence

Becoming calm is a prerequisite for relaxation and concentration, and not all that easy. Many groups have to learn it. All group members are seated in a circle of chairs or simply remain at their tables. If there are tables, the group leader says to the group: 'Put your hands on the table. Rest your head on your hands and close your eyes.' Without tables, the leader says only, 'Close your eyes.' Once everybody has become quiet, the leader says to the group, 'Listen to the silence. When, after a little while, I ask you to open your eyes, I want you to tell me what you could hear in the silence.'

Once the group has learned to listen to the silence with their eyes closed, the exercise can be extended. For example, the leader may open a window or door, and ask group members to listen for noises coming from the outside. Such a silence exercise can also be carried out outside a closed room, for example in the garden or during a walk.

Silence exercises should always be short. Sometimes, children who are very restless may need a long time before they feel able to close their eyes and listen to the silence all by themselves. No child should be criticised because of this. They should simply be asked not to disturb the others. Some adults, too, find it difficult to be quiet with their eyes closed. They require time, as well as the trust of the group, before they are able to participate in this exercise. The group leader can try to record the 'silence' with a tape recorder, and listen to it later with the group. Sometimes it is amazing how 'noisy' silence can be!

28 King of Statues

Everybody freezes in the position they happen to be in at the command of the group leader. The player who does not move for the longest time (the group leader watches closely) is the 'King of Statues' and can be rewarded by, for example, becoming the leader for the next round.

Once the group is familiar with this exercise, it can be carried out again to quickly interrupt restlessness, excitement and the beginning of chaos.

29 Casting a Spell

Players sit or lie on the floor with their eyes closed. The group leader, who is the magician, moves around the room and says in a calm voice, 'I am the magician. I have cast a spell on all of you. You are now asleep. When you feel my magic wand, you will get up and follow me. You are allowed to open your eyes for this'. As a variation on this game, players who have been saved by the magician can hold each other by the hands, and the last player is allowed, in place of the magician, to wake up another player by touching them with their hand.

The game is finished when the 'spell' has been taken off all players.

30 Fantasy Journey

Group members sit comfortably and relaxed on their chairs. Everybody closes their eyes. The leader sends them on a 'fantasy journey' by telling them the following story, in a calming voice: 'You are lying in a meadow … The sun is shining warm on to your body … You can hear the birds sing … There is a pleasant scent of grass … '. In between sentences, the leader allows time so that the group members can think themselves into the setting described. After a while, the leader calls them back into reality by saying, for example: 'The sun is setting slowly … You have to get home … Have a big stretch and open your eyes … You are back with us in the group again.'

There are numerous variations on this exercise. After the two introductory sentences – 'You are lying in a meadow … The sun is shining warm on to your body' – attention can be directed onto other experiences. For example: 'You can see a butterfly … You can smell a flower … You can feel the moss beneath you … You can hear a little stream running nearby … A bee is humming …'.

The exercise can also be expanded: 'You are beginning to look around a little … There is a path at the end of the meadow … You follow the path for a little while … You get to a small forest … You can smell the pines …'.

It is important that, at the end of the exercise, all players are called back gently into reality from the fantasy journey, and that everybody who wants to is given some time to recall experiences from their journey, or even to paint them.

31 Journey of Recovery

All players are sitting comfortably with their eyes closed. They are breathing deeply and calmly in and out. The leader begins by saying: 'Imagine you have really exerted yourselves and now you are exhausted. You desperately need some rest. In your thoughts, you can travel to any place in the world, even to places that don't exist in reality, that you only imagine: for example, to the land of milk and honey, to the place where the fairies live, to the centre of the Earth, and so on. Dream yourselves to any place you like, make yourselves comfortable there, have a rest, enjoy the quiet, the security, the peace.'

After two or three minutes, the leader calls group members back home from their journey: 'Now you feel calm and well rested. You are looking forward to coming home. Return slowly, open your eyes and here you are, back with the group again.'

Afterwards, whoever likes to should be given an opportunity to tell about their experiences during the journey. Initially, this may be easiest in small, familiar sub-groups; later, it may be tried with the whole group. When a group has already done this exercise a few times, it can also be carried out, without a following conversation, simply as a conclusion to a group session, or at the end of the day.

32 Picture Meditation

All group members adopt as comfortable a position as possible and close their eyes. The leader now suggests a fantasy image and helps them to consciously experience themselves and their bodies by providing concrete pointers. For example, the leader may say, 'Imagine you are a rose bush.' After a while, using a calm voice, he provides more pointers, such as: 'Where are you growing? What is the earth like? Try to feel your roots. How deep down in the earth are they? Try to find them. What does your stem feel like? What do your branches feel like? Your leaves? Have you got many flowers? What do they smell like? What colour are they?', and so on.

What and how much information is provided by the leader depends on the group. The group should not be too big for this exercise, and individual group members should already know each other well. After completing this meditation, there should be sufficient time to talk about experiences.

Of course, instead of the rose bush, the leader can also offer different fantasy pictures – for example, an apple tree, a particular animal, a special stone, a house with many rooms, and so on.

(33) Growing

All group members are plants that are growing from seeds. They get bigger and bigger, ripen and then wilt.

Following the instructions of the group leader, everybody initially curls up into seeds and then begins slowly to grow and become bigger and bigger. Once the plants are fully grown, they turn towards the sun, stretch, stand in full ripeness and then begin slowly to wilt. One after the other, they collapse into themselves again, falling on to the floor.

Some groups manage the movements of growing and wilting better when this is accompanied by music.

Instead of plants growing and wilting, one can also perform the opening of a flower in the morning, and the closing in the evening; the slow coming to life and dying down again of a fire; the approach, arrival and departure of a storm, and so on.

(34) **Sound Chain**

Players move freely around the room. One player 'sets the tone'; that is, they hum a tone or make some sort of noise. They can pass on this tone to another player by touching them. The first player is then freed from that tone and can introduce a new one. Every player who has been passed a tone can pass this tone on and continue to produce new tones so that, in the end, all players have a tone.

It can also be agreed that tones can be passed on to players who are already humming a tone. They then have to stop that tone and take on the new one. This way, the noise in the group will change continuously. Talking is not allowed during this exercise.

35) Where is the Noise Coming from?

The group is seated in a circle and everybody closes their eyes. The leader produces a sound somewhere in the room, by, for example, using a ruler to tap the window sill, the window, a wall, a tin, a book, and so on.

The group has to guess how the different noises have been produced. The person who has guessed correctly becomes leader of the next round.

36 Listen Closely

Players are seated in a circle and point with outstretched arms at the leader. Then they close their eyes. The leader begins to walk quietly around the room so that the players can just hear him. Therefore everybody has to be very quiet. Players have to try to track the walk of the leader with outstretched arms. At the leader's command, they get up as quietly as possible and try to follow him, still with their eyes closed. The leader has to act in such a way that the players can just hear him and there is no danger that they may stumble or run into something during their 'blind' walk.

This game is suitable for only a relatively small group who have already had some experience with other stillness and trust exercises.

After completion of the exercise, group members must be given an opportunity to talk about their feelings during the 'blind walk' and intense listening.

(37) Sound Snake

Players close their eyes. They then move freely around the room to the rhythm of a sound source, such as a hand drum or triangle, operated by the leader.

Instead of walking around the room on their own, players can also walk around in pairs or small groups, or the whole group can hold hands and walk around the room to the rhythm of the sounds produced by the leader. The exercise can also be carried out as a pairs exercise, where one player has to keep their eyes open and lead the other player around the room without touching another player.

Advanced groups that are not too big can also form a 'human snake', where everybody except the first person has their eyes closed and has to trust 'blindly' that the head of the snake is leading them safely around the room.

38 Hearing Like a Cat

The group agrees on a mouse noise: for example, a loud squeak, that will immediately wake any sleeping cat. Then all players close their eyes and put their heads on the table: they are all 'sleeping cats'.

The leader now produces a range of different noises: Closing a door, dropping a bag, rattling a bunch of keys, and so on. All these noises fail to disturb the cats' sleep.

However, if the leader produces the agreed 'mouse noise', all cats have to wake up immediately. Whoever wakes up or even twitches at the wrong noise drops out, or can take over from the leader.

(39) Personal Call

The group divides into pairs. Each pair agrees a personal 'call': a sound or a word that needs to be as unusual as possible, so as to stand out from the calls of the other pairs. The pairs then split up and all players are blindfolded. Now, with only their call to help them, they have to try to find their partners. Other noises are not allowed. In no case must players speak, and deliberate touching is also banned. After a previously agreed period of time, which should not be too long, players take off their blindfolds at the leader's word. Those players who are found together in pairs can, for example, be given a point, but the game can also be played without any scoring. It is important that, after the game, time is allowed for discussion among the group members.

40 The Right Way

Using chalk, a path consisting of two lines approximately 20 centimetres apart is marked out on the floor, as winding as possible and including a couple of obstacles, such as an overturned chair, a low bench, and so on. One after the other, players now walk along this path; they are not allowed to step outside the lines defining it.

Players can also walk along the path in pairs. They hold each other's hands; one player could also be blindfolded. Without being able to talk, the leading player has to try to prevent his 'blind' partner from straying off the path or touching an obstacle.

The group leader, or the remaining group members, note down the number of faults and the 'walk' time. The winner is the one who managed to walk without error along the path in the shortest time.

(41) Ships in the Fog

Half of the players are 'passenger ships'. They have to walk carefully around the room with their eyes closed, without colliding with other ships. The other half of the players are ships with fog-horns. With their eyes open, they have to accompany the passenger ships and warn them of the danger of collision by sounding their horns. During this, they are not allowed to touch the passenger ship assigned to them, or to make themselves noticeable by speaking. If it nevertheless comes to a collision, accompanying 'vessels' are out, together with the passenger ships for which they were responsible.

42   Relay of Trust

The group divides into pairs. One partner from each pair stands behind a chair; the other stands opposite the chair some distance away, blindfolded. The partner standing behind the chair now has to direct the blindfolded partner by calling them so that they sit on the chair as quickly and safely as possible.

After the first round, the leader can place some obstacles on the course, so that the 'blind' negotiation of the course is made more difficult, and the standing partner has to give particularly good directions. The blindfolded player also needs a high level of concentration because all seeing callers are allowed to call at the same time, like this: 'Susie, please take one small forward step', 'John, take two big steps forward', 'Anita, take two small steps to the left'. And all that at the same time.

Winners are the pair whose 'blind' partner sits on the chair first.

To make the game manageable, the group must not be too big. Individual players need to know each other well already, and to trust each other, in order for them to agree to a 'blind' walk.

43 Making the Deaf Hear

The group divides into pairs. One partner of each pair covers their ears tightly, so that they cannot hear anything. They are the 'deaf' partner.

Using only gesture, the other partner now tries to describe a piece of music being played, or a verbal message, to their 'deaf' counterpart. After a little while, the 'deaf' partner takes their hands from their ears and describes what they had 'heard'.

Then partners change roles.

Afterwards, there should be an opportunity to exchange experiences within the whole group.

(**44**) Talking Hands 1

Players are seated in pairs opposite each other. They close their eyes. In turn, each tries to communicate a message to the other, using their hands only: for example: 'I am happy', 'I am angry', and so on.

Then they open their eyes again and tell each other what message they have received and what message was actually sent.

At the end, there should be an opportunity to exchange experiences made in pairs with the whole group.

(45) Talking Hands 2

Players find themselves a partner and stand or sit opposite them. They put the palms of their hands on each other and close their eyes. The leader tells a story, such as the following:

'Imagine your hands are meeting on the street; they are pleased to meet and tell each other something funny. All of a sudden, a car sounds its horn and they get a big fright and become really anxious because something appears to have happened at the corner of the street. The hands whisper to each other. All of a sudden, they are in a rush: the bus is arriving. Quickly, they give each other a hug and part.'

While the leader is telling the story, players have to try to let their partner feel the events in the story with their hands. At the end of the game, there has to be sufficient time for individual group members to talk about their experiences if they want to.

46 Sticks

The group divides into pairs, where the two members of each pair are of approximately equal height. Each pair receives a stick, for example an unsharpened pencil. Using counter pressure, players now have to hold this stick between their finger tips or the palms of their hands. A leader then sets tasks that the partners have to carry out while carrying the stick between them; for example, climbing over the waste paper bin, turning around in a circle, sitting down, and so on.

Before the game begins, players can agree that pairs that drop their stick will have to sit out during the next task.

47 Who has Touched You?

All except five players are seated in a circle and have their eyes closed. The five players move around in the middle of the circle. Each of them now touches one of the seated players with their hand: for example, stroking their hair, touching them on the shoulder, pinching them (gently) on the cheek, and so on. After that, the five return to the middle of the circle. The players seated in the circle open their eyes. Those players who felt a touch now have to find out which of the five has touched them. Whoever guesses correctly is allowed into the middle of the circle for the next round.

The group should not be too big, and the game should not be repeated too often, otherwise those players who have nothing to do may easily become restless and unhappy.

Afterwards, the group should talk about their experiences during the game, because hidden feelings may have been set free in some group members through their having been touched.

48 Give Me Your Hand

All players stand in a circle, spaced so that they can all easily touch their neighbour. They close their eyes. The group leader, who is part of the circle, begins to pass around a touch – for example, a hand shake, a pat on the shoulder, a stroke on the cheek, and so on. When the touch has returned to the leader, the word is given for everybody to open their eyes.

Again, it is important here to allow for an opportunity afterwards to talk about the game.

49 Showing Feelings

Players sit on their chairs or on the floor. The leader switches off the light, and the players are allowed to move around as they like in the darkened room. When the light is switched back on, they have to freeze their movements. Once everybody is familiar with the procedure, the leader names feelings during the darkness phase that the players have to express silently as soon as the light comes on: grief, passion, happiness, hope, curiosity, and so on. Groups that have had little practice in this game should not be asked for too much. The game should be quickly brought to an end when players start to mess around or become restless.

After the exercise, time should be given to talk about how difficult it is to express feelings without speech; which feelings were most difficult to express, and what individual players felt during the exercise.

 **50** Epidemic

The group stands or sits in a circle. One of the players pulls a face, and turns to the neighbour on their left. That person now has to make the same 'grimace' and, again, turn to their left neighbour, who in turn has to copy the grimace, and so on. Once they have taken on the grimace, everybody has to maintain this expression until it has reached the last player. If every player has imitated their predecessor only, the last and the first player will – despite all efforts – look considerably different!

In addition, or instead of a 'grimace', other body movements or positions can also be passed on, as true to the original as possible.

51) Who is the Tallest?

Five to 10 players are arranged in a line according to their height by the rest of the group, who have been blindfolded. Depending on the number of group members, the game can also be played as a competition between sub-groups.

The greater the number of players that have to be arranged according to their height, and the more similar they are in terms of their height, the more difficult the game becomes.

52   **Speechless Birthday Line**

The group leader gives the following instruction: 'Please try to arrange yourselves according to the day and month of your birthday. You are not allowed to speak, but you are allowed to give each other as many signs as you want – for example, nodding your head, shaking your head, indicating numbers using your fingers, and so on.'

The completed line is then checked for accuracy by everybody calling out their date of birth.

The game can be made more difficult by adding the year of birth as a further requirement.

Smaller children should initially try to arrange themselves according to height, or length of hair, or shoe size – naturally, without speaking.

(53) Kneading Lumps of Clay

Half the group turns into 'lumps of clay'; the other half become sculptors, who shape the 'lumps of clay' into prescribed statues: for example, into a football team on the playing field; into stall-holders at a busy weekly market, into surgeons in an operating theatre, and so on. While this is going on, the 'lumps of clay' have to try to guess what the sculptors are trying to shape them into.

As a variation, the 'lumps of clay' can let themselves be shaped while they have their eyes closed, and again have to try to guess what they are supposed to portray. Of course, a number of sculptors can work on one 'lump of clay'. Another variation is to have 'blind' sculptors who have to try to copy a model statue that has already been created by another sculptor from a 'lump of clay', using new 'lumps of clay'.

(54) Master Builder

The players are divided into two groups of equal size. Using any items available in the room, such as tables, chairs, bins and books, and without making any noise or exchanging any words, the first group now has to create a construction. The group leader uses a stopwatch to measure the time taken.

The second group then has to take down the construction, also without making any noise, and without letting anything collapse. Again, the time is recorded. Whoever wants to can declare the faster group to be the winners. Alternatively, everybody can get involved in creating a historical monument, and then taking it down again, as quickly and as quietly as possible.

Every player should have at least one turn at building up and taking down.

(55) Blind Cashier

Players are seated in a circle, keeping their eyes closed. One at a time, the leader passes around a few coins. Using their sense of touch only, the players have to find out the value of the individual coins and, finally, the sum total of the coins that have passed through their hands. Of course, they are only allowed to say their results aloud once all coins have found their way back to the leader and the leader has said the words, 'Open your eyes'. To be extra mean, the leader can smuggle in a foreign coin.

The game becomes easier if players are given an opportunity to handle the coins with open eyes before it starts, and when the number of players and coins is not too large. Instead of using coins, this game can also be played by players having to identify all sorts of objects using only their sense of touch. The leader can then ask either for the names of individual objects, or for a category heading: for example, tools, contents of a trouser pocket, and so on.

The more unusual the category heading, the more difficult the game becomes.

56 Silent Post (Chinese Whispers)

A secret word is whispered from ear to ear, while the group is seated in a circle or maintains its normal seating arrangements. The last receiver of this 'silent post' says the word aloud. Then players are allowed to send a new 'silent post'.

The game becomes more difficult when, instead of a single word, a whole sentence is passed on. The sentence should not be too long.

This game requires no preparation at all; can be played quickly, and is well known to everyone. Therefore it is particularly well suited for calming, and for concentrating in between other activities.

57   Silent Post: Through Mime

While the group is seated in a circle, imagined objects, such as a hot saucepan, a stick, a stone, a wet sponge, a bag of ice cubes, and so on, are passed silently, using mime. The last player to receive the mime has to guess the name of the imagined object. If they have guessed correctly, they are allowed to pass on a new object. If they guess wrongly, another player continues, according to a sequence agreed prior to the start of the game.

The game can also be played with any other seating arrangements, without first having to move tables and chairs about.

This game is enjoyed even by adults and, at the same time, leads to a heightened awareness of one's own body and movements.

58 Sending a Telegram

Players create a line by standing or sitting one behind the other. The last player is asked to wire a word or (simple) picture along the line, by using their fingers to 'write' or 'draw' on the back of the person in front of them. As the word or picture is passed forward, players are not allowed to talk, and no other signals are allowed. When the telegram has arrived at the first player in the line, its content is compared with the one originally sent.

The game can also be played as a competition between several groups. The group which was able to concentrate best on tactile impressions is the winner.

59 Who is Conducting the Orchestra?

Players are seated on chairs in a circle. One player is asked to leave the room. In their absence, the group decides on one player to be conductor who, remaining seated, is going to mime playing particular instruments: piano, flute, cello, guitar, violin, and so on. The rest of the group imitates these movements. The player outside is called back into the orchestral rehearsal when the first instrument movement has begun. The leader explains that they have to find out who the conductor is. To do this, they have to watch all players closely, to determine who is causing the changes to the instruments being played.

When the conductor has been recognised, that person has to go outside and a new conductor is chosen.

Instead of playing instruments, other movements can be demonstrated and imitated: clapping hands, stamping feet, wringing arms, rubbing stomachs, and so on. Again, one player will have to guess who is giving the command for a new movement.

60 Where are We Just Now?

Players are spread out randomly across the room. One player is briefly sent outside. The group then agrees on a scenario that they are going to portray together: for example, waiting at the bus stop, going to work on the bus, the beginning of a first dancing lesson, or viewing an exhibition. The scenario is expressed through mime only, and the player who has been called in has to guess what is being mimed.

61 Freeing Prisoners

Players are seated in a circle. In the centre of the circle there is a prison guard with a prisoner. The guard is blindfolded, the prisoner's arms and legs are tied loosely with two scarfs. The players in the circle now have to try to free the prisoner without attracting the attention of the guard.

Afterwards, a new guard and a new prisoner are determined.

62 Trackers on a Hidden Path

One player is appointed to be a 'tracker'. The others sit or stand in a circle, facing outwards. From the centre of the circle, the tracker now tries to creep up to one of the players from behind. If he is noticed by the player, the player raises an arm – turning around is not allowed – and the tracker has to return to the centre of the circle; and then creep up to another player. If he reaches a player without being noticed, this player has to take over as the tracker. If the group is a large one, there can be two or three trackers in the circle, so that a number of players are occupied at the same time. The trackers have to select their victims precisely, to avoid any misunderstandings as to who was being selected by whom. With smaller children, the leader needs to ensure that they don't raise their arms when they have not yet noticed a tracker.

(63) Watchful Dog with Bone

Players are seated in a circle facing the middle, where there is a blindfolded player who is pretending to be a blind dog guarding a bone (any object will do – the most difficult is a bunch of keys). One player from the circle tries to steal the bone. If the dog notices and manages to touch the thief, the thwarted thief has to sit down again and another player is allowed a go. If a player manages to steal the bone, they can be the new guard dog.

64 Little Henry, Say 'Peep'

All but one player are seated in a circle. The remaining player is blindfolded. Before the game starts, all players change seats so that the blindfolded player will not know from memory who was sitting where.

The blindfolded player now has to sit on the lap of any of the players and ask: 'Little Henry, say "peep"'. If they recognise the voice of the person whose knee they are sitting on, they are allowed to pass on the blindfold to this person and take a place in the circle. If they do not recognise the player, they have to try their luck again with another player. Players sitting in the circle should swap seats before each new round.

Subject to agreement prior to the start of the game, hands may be used to help recognise the person 'underneath'.

65 Blind Bridge Attendant

A marked off playing field (not too big) is split into three strips, the middle one being the bridge. On the bridge, there are two or more players who have been blindfolded – the 'blind bridge attendants'. The other players have to spread out equally on to the two outer strips. They have to try to get across the bridge into the other strip without being noticed or even caught by the 'blind' attendants. Prisoners are turned into 'blind' assistants to the bridge attendants, so that it becomes increasingly difficult to cross the bridge without being noticed. During the game, things need to be kept extremely quiet so that the bridge attendants stand some chance of noticing frontier crossers and, at the same time, frontier crossers do not run the danger of being caught too quickly.

Kim's Games

(66) Memory Test ('Looking' Kim)

In this standard form of all Kim's games, players are required to remember as many items as possible from a selection of small objects. Depending on the age of the players, the leader puts 10 to 30 small objects, such as a ballpoint, pencil, rubber, ruler, tea spoon, cork, scissors, handkerchief or keys, on a table. Every player is allowed to look at them for two to three minutes. Then they are covered, and players have to recall what they can remember by, for example, writing down as many of the items as they can remember in a given time.

Afterwards, lists are compared with the actual collection of objects.

If the group is only a small one, players can put their memory skills to the test one at a time by recalling orally the items they can remember. Obviously, if this option is used, the collection of objects has to be varied for each player.

67 There Must be Order ('Order' Kim)

A board from a board game, such as chess, Ludo, Nine Men's Morris, or Scrabble® is put on the table. Five to 10 counters such as corks, coins or Scrabble® letters are spread out on it.

All players are now allowed an equal amount of time to look at the board and remember how the counters are arranged on it. Then the board is covered or carried out of the room, and everybody has to do a sketch of the board and the counters arrangement. When everybody has finished, the sketches are compared to the original.

The game becomes easier when players have to recall only the order of the counters, without having to remember their value. In other words, the arrangement of the chess pieces (for example) must be right in terms of which squares have pieces on them, but it does not matter whether the pieces are a queen, a pawn or a castle.

68 There is Something Wrong at the Smiths' House ('Observation' Kim 1)

All players are asked to leave the room for a brief period. During this time, the leader makes a few changes in the room – for example, taking down or moving some pictures, swapping some chairs around, moving the standard lamp to another corner of the room, switching lights on or off, drawing or opening curtains, removing the table cloth, and so on. Then players are called back into the room, and have to find out what has been changed. Of course, the group could also decide to send only one player out of the room.

(69) False Blossoms
('Observation' Kim 2)

Kim's games can also be played outdoors. The leader makes about 10 changes along a short stretch of path that could not occur naturally. For example, the leader puts a rose in the holly bush, a daisy in the apple tree, an apple in the hedge, a paper violet among real violets, and so on. Afterwards, the other players have to try to discover the 'false blossoms'.

The game becomes easier when the leader tells players how many changes they are looking for.

(70) Who has Changed?
('People-Observation' Kim 1)

Players are seated in a circle. One player is asked to carefully study the other players, and is then sent outside. While the player is out of the room, changes are made to two or three players: for example, a necklace is taken off, a hairstyle is changed, a jacket is put on. The player is then called back in and has to try to discover what has changed.

The game becomes easier if changes are allowed to take place only in a particular area – for example, only around the head, the upper body or the feet – and the player is told how many changes they are supposed to be looking for.

71 Fashion Espionage ('People-Observation' Kim 2)

The group is divided into two groups of equal size, and every player is given a partner. Initially, players are not told what they will have to do later, but are told to introduce themselves, to chat, and to observe their partner carefully.

After about three minutes, one player from each pair is sent outside. The players who are left in the room are given pen and paper, and are asked to write down in as much detail as possible what their respective conversation partners were wearing.

After the other players have been called back into the room, the fashion espionage reports are read out loud and are compared with the actual clothes. Depending on what has been agreed prior to the game, the player who provides the most detailed description can be declared the winner.

72 Recognising Noises ('Listening' Kim)

All players sit at a table and are given pen and paper. Behind a curtain, the leader has laid out a collection of objects that can be used to make noises: for example, a bunch of keys, a ball, a ruler, a comb, and so on. Players are asked to write down any noises that they recognise, but are not allowed to speak while the leader is producing the different noises. After five to 10 noises, the players' answers are compared with the actual noises. With smaller children, it is best to compare results immediately after each noise.

Relatively easy to guess are the following noises: bouncing a ball, tearing fabric, opening a bottle, cracking nuts, bursting a blown-up paper bag, or setting off an alarm clock.

More difficult to guess are noises such as blowing up a balloon, pumping up a bicycle tyre, striking a match, crunching paper, brushing off shoes, pouring water, brushing teeth, gargling or rubbing down a piece of wood using sandpaper. Noises to be guessed can, of course, be recorded and played on a tape recorder. Environmental sounds, such as engine noise from a car or aeroplane, sawing wood, footsteps, typing, running a tap, bowling alley sounds, and so on, can be pre-recorded and played to the group as a recognition task. Characteristic sounds can also be recorded with the help of props. Here the game can be made more difficult, with the recording technique having to be guessed as well. You can also use commercially available sound tapes, which are offered by a number of educational suppliers.

(73) Feely Bag ('Touch' Kim 1)

The leader puts some small objects in a bag or pillow case: paper clips, a pair of (blunt) scissors, keys, corks, a pen, a rubber, a bottle opener, and so on. Players are seated in a circle and reach into the bag one at a time to try to recognise an object by feeling it. After they have named an object, they take it out of the bag to check whether they have guessed correctly.

As a variation, a player may be allowed to continue to feel and take out objects from the bag for as long as they are guessing correctly. When they make a mistake, it is the next player's turn, and so on, until the bag is empty.

(74) Seeing Hands ('Touch' Kim 2)

Everybody is seated in a circle. The leader blindfolds one player at a time, and gives them an object that they have to guess by feeling it. Younger children can be given objects such as a ball, a scarf, or a book; older children, teenagers, or adults can be given more complicated objects, such as a camera, a stapler, a hole punch, and so on.

Of course, there has to be a different item for each player, and items need to be kept hidden under a cloth or in a box.

As a variation, all players seated in the circle can be asked to close their eyes at the same time, or they can sit around a table that is covered with a big table cloth. Everybody has to hide their hands under the table cloth. The leader then passes around a number of items – for example, a nail brush, a wet sponge, a dry or slimy bar of soap, a conker with or without its spiky shell, a piece of fur, and so on.

Each object has to be passed silently from hand to hand as quickly as possible. As soon as it has arrived back with the leader, each player writes down what they think they have felt. After a previously agreed number of rounds, answers are read out and compared with the actual items.

This variation of the game facilitates concentration, but above all it is good fun. For this reason, it is particularly well suited to rounding off a more 'serious' work session.

(75) Who am I? ('Person Touch' Kim)

Players are seated in a circle. One player is blindfolded. Their task is to recognise the other players through touch only. Before the player can start, the person they are going to identify by touch needs to be changed a little. For example, they put on a hat, take off their glasses, stick on a beard, remove their ear-rings, wear a scarf, and so on. No words may be exchanged during the game. The game should be brought to an end if the blindfolded player is unable to make out the identity of the person they are trying to guess after a previously agreed amount of time, because the game will become too stressful for the blindfolded player, and too boring for everybody else. In that case, you need to begin again, but this time the player who is to be identified should be changed less.

76 Nose ('Smell' Kim)

The leader prepares 10 to 15 containers with different 'scents'. All containers need to look identical, and must be covered with opaque lids with holes in them, so that players cannot recognise the content by sight.

In the containers you can put, pepper, cheese, soap powder, coffee, perfume, vanilla essence, and so on.

One after the other, players smell the containers and write down what they think they have smelled. When everybody has smelled each one, the containers are opened, and their contents are compared with the players' notes.

With small children, it is a good idea to pass around one container at a time for everybody to smell, and then talk about the right answer immediately afterwards.

A variation would be to prepare two equal sets of containers and ask players to pair up containers with the same smells.

(77) Juice Bar ('Taste' Kim)

Five to 10 different juices or other drinks are poured into glasses or beakers that all look the same, arranged in a line next to each other. In the glasses can be, for example, water, cherry juice, lemon juice, orange juice, elderberry juice, carrot juice, tomato juice, milk, apple juice, grapefruit juice, drinking yogurt, and so on.

Now, one after the other, blindfolded players sample each drink, all in the same order. (The players should each be given a straw with which to drink.)

After each sampling, players write down what they have tasted. Afterwards, they are allowed to look at the drinks and compare them with their own results.

(78) Daily News ('Knowledge' Kim)

Together, the group listens to or watches the news on the radio or television, after which the leader sends all players out of the room, and calls them back in one-by-one. Each has to answer three to 10 questions related to the news: for example, what was the name of the *first* politician that was named, which piece of news came from the United States, what is the weather going to be like tomorrow? Of course, the wording of the questions has to be the same for each player. The player who answers the most, or all, questions correctly is the winner.

Such 'knowledge' Kim's games can also be played following the reading of news, short stories, recipes, DIY instructions, and so on.

Attention &

Thinking Games

79 All Birds are Flying High

Players are seated at tables, ideally arranged in a large circle or in a square, but in any case in such a way that everybody can see everybody else. Everybody drums on the table with their fingers. One player is the leader, who begins:

'All birds are flying high.' – At the same time, the leader's hands go up. All other players also have to raise their hands, because birds do indeed fly. The leader continues:

'All sparrows are flying high' – leader and players raise their hands.
'All aeroplanes are flying high' – everybody raises their hands.
'All elephants are flying high' – the leader's hands go up.

Those players who also raised their hands, instead of continuing to drum on the table, have to drop out: elephants definitely do not fly.

The faster the leader lets things fly, and the more unusual the flying objects become, the more difficult the game will be.

Different game variations are possible. For example:

'All cars go on the road', 'Scooters go on the road', 'Aeroplanes go on the road' (not), 'Rockets go on the road' (not), and so on;

'All fish can swim', 'Sharron Davies can swim', 'Stones can swim' (not), and so on.

Sentences need to be accompanied by appropriate hand movements.

80 Old Opera

Players are seated in a circle. The leader tells them that they have a friend who is a porter for the old opera and will only let in visitors who, in his opinion, are dressed appropriately. Then the leader tells the group what they were wearing for their last visit to the opera, naming an item of clothing worn by the player sitting on their left. For example: 'I went to the opera the other day. I was wearing trainers. The porter was happy to let me in.' Then the leader asks the player on their right: 'What would you wear for your opera visit?' If that player names – by coincidence – an item of clothing worn by the leader, they will be allowed to go to the opera, but if they name something else they will not be allowed in, and they will not be told the reason. The game then moves on to the neighbour to the right of that player, and so on. The leader's task is to say whether or not players are going to be allowed to enter the old opera. Those players who have found out what admittance criteria the porter is using continue to play, and try to make the other players even more uncertain by naming either items of clothing that are very difficult to discover, or particularly 'normal' items of clothing. The game can be played until everybody has found out what criteria the porter is using to decide whether someone is allowed into the opera, or not.

As a variation, the item of clothing could be worn by the respective right-hand neighbour, or by any player in the circle, with the latter variation being especially difficult.

81 Noah's Ark

The group is seated in a circle. One player begins: 'Noah takes two sparrows on to the ark, chirp chirp.' The player to their right continues: 'Noah takes two sparrows on to the ark, chirp chirp, and two pigs, oink oink', and so on.

Each player has to repeat all the animals and their noises that have already been named, and add a new pair with corresponding sounds. Anybody who makes a mistake, or who cannot remember the whole sequence, has to sit out for one round.

Animal noises can also be imitated by all the players together, except, of course, the new noise, which they do not yet know. The game becomes more difficult when not just a noise, but also a characteristic movement has to be added and repeated. For example, 'Noah takes two sparrows on to the ark, chirp chirp.' is accompanied by the player using their hands to mime the opening and closing of a bird's beak; 'Noah takes two sparrows on to the ark, chirp chirp' – beak movement – 'and two pigs, oink oink.' At the same time, the player moves their fist in front of their nose, pretending to have a pig's nose. And so on.

82 Zoo Visit

Players are seated in a circle and two, three or four players at a time – depending on the size of the group – are given an animal name: panther, whale, monkey, parrot, sea-horse, and so on. The leader stands in the middle and tells a zoo story which features, from time to time, two of the animal types that have been given to the group. For example:

'Every morning, Joe the zoo keeper starts his day by preparing breakfast for the whale and monkeys; only after that is it the panthers' and parrots' turn. Once everybody has had their breakfast, the whale and sea horses get fresh water.' And so on.

As soon as players' animal names are mentioned, they have to quickly swap chairs and the leader has to try to get a chair. The player who is left over becomes the new leader, and continues to tell the story. If they use the word 'zoo', everybody has to stand up and swap chairs.

The game becomes more difficult if the leader does not just name individual animals, but uses categories, where all animals that come under that heading have to change places. For example, if the leader said the word 'bird', the parrot and any other bird in the circle would have to change places; if the leader said 'all animals beginning with "p"', it would be the turn of the panther, the parrots and all other animals whose names begin with 'p'.

Instead of zoo animals, one could also play 'fruit in a fruit bowl', or 'tools in a tool box', and so on.

83 Bad Seven

Seating arrangements are irrelevant, as players only need to know in which order they are going to take turns. The group counts: one, two, three, four, five, six, psst, eight, nine, and so on. All numbers are said out aloud except seven, multiples of seven (14, 21, 28, and so on), and all numbers that contain the number 7 (17, 27, and so on), where the respective player has to say 'psst'. Anyone who makes a mistake has to drop out, and has to show that they are out by folding their arms in front of them. The game can also be played with any other number but seven.

For younger players, who may not be that confident with their times tables, the game can be made easier by only asking them to say 'psst' for numbers that obviously contain the number 7 (7, 17, 27 and so on).

(84) Choir Practice

The group sings simple songs, whose words are familiar to most people. To make sure everybody knows the words, you can go through them once beforehand. One person is the leader. Before every song, the leader sets a task: for example, 'All monosyllabic nouns have to be replaced by "boom".' Or specific words are omitted altogether: for example, all definite articles are left out, so players have to sing 'boom' for every 'the' in the song. The more conditions set, the more difficult and the more fun the song becomes.

The game can also be made more difficult by speeding up the tempo of the song.

85 This is My Elbow

Players are seated in a circle. The leader walks up to one of the players, touches their own nose and says: 'This is my elbow.' The player who has been addressed now has to react in exactly the opposite way; touching their elbow and saying: 'This is my nose.'

If they have responded correctly, the leader turns to another player, touches, for example, their own knee and says: 'This is my ear.' In response, the player opposite has to touch their ear and say: 'This is my knee.'

Whoever makes a mistake becomes the new leader. This game could be much more fun if players who have responded correctly become the new leader.

In another variation, the leader touches the other player's nose and says: 'This is my elbow.' The player who has been addressed then has to touch the leader's elbow and say: 'This is my nose.' The faster the pace of the game, the more concentration is called for, in order to react correctly.

86　Floppy has Lost His Hat

Each player is given a number, which they have to remember. One player is Floppy, and they start the following conversation: 'Floppy has lost his hat. Number 7 has got it.' The player who has number 7 answers: 'Who, me?' Floppy confirms: 'Yes, you.' Number 7 says: 'Not me. Number 5 has got it.' The player with the number 5 asks: 'Who, me?' Again, Floppy confirms: 'Yes, you.' Number 5 says: 'Not me. Number 3 has got it', and so on.

The faster the conversation goes, the more difficult the game becomes, and the more concentration is required from the players.

87 One Duck with Two Legs: Splash

Players are seated in a circle, and speak one after the other: Player 1: 'One duck'; Player 2: 'with two legs'; Player 3: 'jumps into the water'; Player 4: 'Splash.' The fifth player has to clap their hands once. The sixth player continues: 'Two ducks'; Player 7: 'with four legs'; Player 8: 'jump into the water; Player 9: 'Splash, splash.' The tenth player has to clap twice. The eleventh player continues: 'Three ducks' – and so on.

For a change, it could of course be four-legged dogs, or three-legged robots, or one-legged storks, and so on, who jump into the water.

88   A Long Sentence

The players sit in a circle. One player begins with a two-word sentence, for example: 'Nicola walks.' The player to their left lengthens the sentence by one word; for example: 'Nicola walks slowly.' The third player adds another word: 'Nicola walks very slowly.' The fourth player adds yet another word: 'Nicola walks very slowly uphill.' And so on, until no player can think of another word to extend the sentence. Whoever makes a mistake or cannot think of a word simply misses out on their turn.

The game lasts longer if the forming of subordinate sentences is allowed. However, it should be agreed before the game starts whether a new word always has to be added to the end of the sentence, or whether players will be allowed to add a word anywhere in the sentence – as demonstrated by the third player in our example.

89 Family Miller

All players are members of the Miller family. At the beginning of the game, roles are allocated. The first player is father Miller, the second mother Miller, the third is son Max Miller, the fourth is daughter Maria Miller, the fifth grandfather Miller, and so on. If the group is a big one, characters like the dog, Rover Miller, the cat, Mitzy Miller, the parrot, Polly Miller, and so on can also take part. One group member becomes the family historian, who tells a story about the family Miller, in which the names of all family members are mentioned as often as possible. Players have to pay close attention, because, every time their name is mentioned, they have to stand up and bow. When the player says, 'family Miller', everybody has to stand up and bow; when they say, 'parents Miller', only father and mother Miller stand up, and so on.

Of course, the story can also be about the family Smith, Harris or Bloggs. Instead of talking about a family, a player could also talk about a debate in the House of Commons, be a person reporting on a headmasters' conference, a village farmer's wife talking about the farmers' wives' AGM, and so on.

The game can be played without having winners and losers, just for fun and to facilitate more attentive listening. Of course, it could be agreed that any family member who does not pay attention has to drop out. Whoever is left over in the end becomes the new rapporteur. The faster they can talk, the more difficult and the more fun the whole game becomes.

90 Fish in the Pond

The group is seated around a large table, or in a circle on the floor. Between the players, on the table or on the floor, a pond is marked out, using a piece of rope or some chalk. One player is the leader and gives the commands.

If the leader says 'Right', all players must put their right hand in front of them, without touching the outside or inside of the pond. If they say 'Left', all players have to put their left hand in front of them. At the word 'Middle', they have to put both hands in front of them. Only at the word 'Pond' must they put their hands in the pond.

The game commands more attention the faster commands follow each other.

91 Slapping Hands

The players are seated in a circle around a table. Hands are put flat on the table in such a way that everybody's right hand is placed over their neighbour's left hand on the table.

Once all hands are placed in the circle as described above, the game can begin. One player, who is the leader, slaps the table once with their right hand. This means that in that direction – that is, to the right – one player after the other slaps the table with their right hand. As soon as one player in the circle slaps the table twice, the direction has to be changed and the game continues around to the left: one after the other, players now slap their left hand on the table. As soon as the next player slaps the table twice, the direction of slapping is changed again. If someone makes a mistake, they only drop out with the hand that has made the mistake. The other hand is allowed to continue slapping. This game requires a high level of concentration and provides a lot of fun, especially because players' hands are put on top of each other, and players have to pay exact attention as to whether it is their own hand or the right or left hand of their neighbour that needs to slap.

The faster the slapping, and the more often the direction is changed, the more difficult the game becomes.

92 Hands Off

All players are seated around a table, and everybody puts their hands on their knees. When the leader says, 'Attention!', everybody puts their hands on the table, with their thumbs up. If the leader says, 'Rest', everybody puts their thumbs down and hands lie flat on the table. If the leader says 'Hands off', all hands have to return to knees.

The faster commands are given, the more difficult the game becomes. It can also be made even more difficult by adding further commands. At 'Left, march' for example, all players have to put their left hand only flat on the table, at 'Right, march' only their right hand, and so on.

93 Main Sender – Minor Sender

Players stand or are seated in a circle. The 'main sender' raises both hands to head height. Their neighbours on the left and right, who are 'minor senders', hold up their hand that is nearest to the main sender, also at head height. Main sender and minor senders now begin 'sending' at the same time, by waving with raised hands: the main sender says their name and the name of the player they are sending to.

For example:

> 'Main sender Peter calling main sender Sue.' Main sender Sue and her two minor senders have to receive immediately by also raising and waving their hands. If they have responded correctly to the radio signal, the addressed main sender and her minor senders are allowed to send a new message to another 'main sender with minor senders'.

If someone does not react, or reacts incorrectly, they have to drop out for that round, stay in the circle and clearly signal that they are 'out' by crossing their arms in front of them. The players remaining in the game have to be careful: they will sometimes have to function as a minor sender across one or several players who have dropped out. Therefore the game demands greater and greater attention. It also becomes more difficult, the faster the radio messages follow each other.

94　My Name is Britta and I do it Like This

The group is seated in a circle. One player begins by saying, 'My name is Britta and I do it like this' – and with this the player makes any movement, for example, they could scratch behind their left ear with their left hand. The player's neighbour to the left now continues: 'Your name is Britta and you do it like this' – scratches behind their left ear with their left hand – 'and my name is Billy and I do it like this' – he lifts his right leg horizontally into the air. Billy's left-hand neighbour now has to repeat Billy's name and his movement and then add their own name and a new movement, and so on.

One after the other, each player has to repeat the name and movement of the previous player, and add their name with a further, new movement.

The game becomes more difficult – and should only be played like this in small groups – if every player has to repeat all previous names and movements.

95 Simon Says

The group choose a leader around whom they form a loose circle. They now have to follow all of the leader's commands, in such a way that they always copy what the leader does, but not what is said.

For example, if the leader says: 'Simon says, "Kneel down!"', and kneels down, everybody has to kneel down, too. However, if the leader says: 'Simon says, "Kneel down!"', but remains standing, all other players must also remain standing.

The game can also be played the other way around: players must always do what the leader says, regardless of what they do.

The faster the commands follow each other, the more difficult – and funnier – the game becomes.

96 | I Spy with My Little Eye

One player thinks of something in the room that is visible to everybody, and lets other players guess what it is, by providing more and more information about it. Whoever calls out the name of the item in question is allowed to think of the next item to be guessed.

For example, the player thinks of the red candlestick on the table and says: 'I spy with my little eye something that is red.' Someone guesses: 'Peter's red jumper.' Answer: 'No, far too soft, I see something harder.' And so on.

It may be best to ask players to write down the item they originally thought of before guessing begins, so no one is tempted to let players continue guessing even though they have already guessed correctly.

97 Hospital

Players and the leader are seated in a circle. After a few players have been sent out of the room, the leader explains the game to the others. They are not allowed to answer any question that is addressed directly to them, but instead have to answer the immediately preceding question that was addressed to another player. The first waiting player is now called back into the room. The leader explains that the player has entered a hospital, and that it is their task to find out the illness of the patients. To do this, the player has to ask one player after the other one question. For example, the player then asks one of the 'patients', 'How old are you?' The person who has been asked remains quiet, until the player moves on to the next 'patient': 'What is your name?' This 'patient' now answers: '12.' The player turns to the third 'patient': 'What colour is your jumper?' The 'patient' answers: 'Elisabeth'. When the player has finally discovered what illness the 'patients' are suffering from, the next waiting player is called in.

98 Clap Ball

All players stand or are seated in a circle. In the middle of the circle, there is a player with a ball, which they throw to any of the other players. That player has to clap their hands before they catch the ball, and then throw it back to the player in the middle. Whoever forgets to clap their hands, or could not catch the ball, has to drop out. (Alternatively, they can continue to play under more difficult conditions: for example, by having to kneel down. With the next ball they manage to catch correctly with a clap, they are 'released' and allowed to stand up or sit down.)

The more skilful the player in the middle is in disguising who they are going to throw the ball to, and the more quickly they throw the ball, the more difficult the game becomes.

99 Clapping

All players are seated in a circle. They count around the circle, and everyone has to remember their number. Then the game begins.

All players slap their upper thighs with their hands, clap their hands in front of their body and snap their fingers, once with their left hand and once with their right. One player, who has been determined prior to the start of the game, calls out their number when snapping the fingers of their right hand, and someone else's number when snapping the fingers of their left hand. The player who has that number has to continue the sequence in the same way.

The pace of the game should be relatively slow, until everyone has mastered the movements. The faster the tempo subsequently becomes, the more difficult the game will become.

(100) Packing a Suitcase

The group is seated in a circle. One player begins packing their suitcase by naming one item that they are putting into it. For example, they say 'I am packing a shirt'. The next player has to repeat that item and add another one: 'I am packing a shirt and trousers'. The third player repeats both items and adds yet another: 'I am packing a shirt, trousers and my tooth brush'. Each player always has to repeat all the items that have already been packed, in the right order, and then add one new one. Thus suitcase packing becomes more difficult from player to player.

Instead of packing a suitcase, the group can fill a fruit basket, catch zoo animals, go shopping for a party, organise a second-hand clothes sale, equip a library, and so on.

If someone makes a mistake, they can drop out for the current round. Whoever puts the last item in the suitcase can choose the topic for the next round of the game, and start off the round.

(101) Commando Pimpernel

The group is seated or stands in a circle. A leader stands in the middle and calls out what the other players have to do. The leader also has to follow each of their own commands. For example, they call out: 'Commando kneel down!' and kneel down. Everybody else also has to kneel down. Then the leader begins to wave and calls out: 'Commando wave!' Now everybody must wave. And so on.

However, if the leader omits the word 'Commando', none of the other players must react: all have to remain totally serious and continue with their current movement. Those players who have not paid any attention have to drop out. Players who have dropped out are only allowed to rejoin the group when the leader calls out: 'Commando Pimpernel!'

The game becomes more difficult, the faster the leader's commands follow each other, and the more surprising and complicated the movements are.

102 Magic Number

The group is seated in a circle and agrees on a 'magic number' – for example, the number 5. Then one player starts off the game by throwing a soft ball, a screwed-up paper ball, or something similarly light to another player, and calling that player's name and any number: for example, 'Peter 1'. Peter catches the ball and repeats: 'One'. Then he throws the ball to another player: 'Sarah 3'. Sarah catches the ball, repeats 'Three', and throws the ball to another player, calling: 'Mary 5'. Because 5 is the magic number, Mary must not catch the ball and must not say 'Five'. She has to remain sitting still and let the ball drop to the floor. Only then is she allowed to pick up the ball and continue the game.

The game becomes more difficult when not only the number 5, but also all multiples of that number, (10, 15, 20, and so on) become 'magic numbers'. Another variation to make the game even more difficult, instead of one number, players agree to have two 'magic numbers' at the same time.

Anyone who makes a mistake has to fold their arms in front of their chest, and must not be called any more. Remaining players have to pay increasingly more attention.

(103) Rhinoceros, Elephant and Duck

Before the game starts, it is explained to everybody how three players who are sitting next to each other can portray a rhinoceros, an elephant and a duck.

For the rhinoceros, the player in the middle mimes a long nose, by putting both hands in front of his face. The other two use their thumbs and index fingers to indicate small rhinoceros ears to the left and right of the player's head. For the elephant, the player in the middle mimes the trunk by touching the nose with one hand and putting the other arm through the circle that has been created. The other two use both arms to shape a pair of large elephant ears. For the duck, the player in the middle mimes a duck's beak, using both hands placed in front of the mouth. The other two stand up and wag their bottoms like ducks.

Now the game can start. All players are seated in a circle. One becomes the leader and goes into the middle of the circle, then points to one of the players and says, for example, 'Elephant'. The player who has been addressed, together with the neighbours to their left and right, now has to mime an elephant, as agreed beforehand. In quick succession, the leader now asks further players to be elephants, rhinoceroses or ducks. The faster the leader gives instructions, the greater the attention required from the other players to ensure that they do not miss their part and do not portray the wrong animal. Anyone who makes a mistake remains seated in the circle with their arms crossed and is not allowed to participate any more. Now the game becomes even more difficult for the other players: they may have to 'complete' a particular animal across one or several players on their left and right.

104 Ribble-Dibble

All players are seated in a circle. Initially, everybody is a 'Ribble-Dibble without a dot'. Counting around the circle begins, starting with any player at number 1, so that now everybody also has a number. And then the actual game begins.

Ribble-Dibble Number 1 starts by calling one of the other players: 'Ribble-Dibble number 1 without a dot is calling Ribble-Dibble number 5 without a dot'. That player then continues: 'Ribble-Dibble number 5 without a dot is calling Ribble-Dibble number 13 without a dot'. If player number 13 now misses their turn through inattention, they are given a dot on the forehead (use a pen or a sticker). They are now Ribble-Dibble number 13 with one dot and are allowed to continue: 'Ribble-Dibble number 13 with one dot is calling Ribble-Dibble number 11 without a dot', and so on.

Players are given black dots for each mistake that they make so that, in the course of the game, there will many different Ribble-Dibbles: those without dots, those with one dot, and those with two, three and more dots. As a result, the game becomes more and more difficult – and funnier. Both difficulty and amusement can be further increased by upping the pace of the game.

(105) Running the Gauntlet

The players position themselves in two lines, in such a way that they create an alleyway approximately one metre wide. At the command of the leader, the two last players of each line have to walk slowly down the alleyway, and have to try not to change their expression. The players forming the alleyway have to try to make the players who are running the gauntlet laugh, by calling out, grimacing or fooling around, but not touching. If they succeed, they have won that particular player as an additional member for their own line.

The team with the most members after everybody has run the gauntlet once is the winner.

(106) Animal Noises

Players are seated in a circle. Each is given the name of an animal: a donkey, a cow, a small dog, a big dog, a pig and so on.

The leader now begins indiscriminately to question individual players. For example: 'What animal are you?', 'How old are you?' and so on. The players being asked are only allowed to answer using their animal voices. For example, under no circumstances may they answer 'a donkey'; they may only reply with their animal voice: 'Eeyore'. Anyone making a mistake crosses their arms and is no longer addressed by the leader during this round. The person left at the end is the new leader.

The game becomes more difficult the faster the leader's questions follow each other, and the more they tempt players to answer with a word or a number instead of an animal noise.

(107) Zipp-Zapp

Zipp-Zapp not only requires concentration, but, at the same time, serves as a 'getting-to-know-each-other' game. All players except one are seated in a circle. The remaining player now takes up a position in front of one of the sitting players and says, 'Zipp'. The player who has been addressed now has to say the name of their right-hand neighbour, or say 'Zapp'; after that they have to say the name of their left-hand neighbour. At 'Zipp-Zapp', all players have to change seats. The player who is left over starts the 'Zipp-Zapp' game all over again.

Concentration
Games for the
Whole Body

(108) Blind Figure of Eight

All players are blindfolded. They hold each other by the hand, and the leader tells them what they have to do. For example, they have to create a star, a circle, an oval, a figure of eight, and so on. When all group members have the feeling that the figure is complete, they communicate with each other and open their eyes.

In larger groups, the game can also be played as a competition between sub-groups. The leader decides which group's figure is closest to the one requested.

(109) Busy Bees

Players form pairs and elect a queen. The queen gives different instructions. For example: 'Shake hands', 'Link arms', 'Stand back to back', 'Look at each other' and so on. However, if the queen calls out, 'Busy bees!', all bee pairs have to split up and 'fly off' to find a new partner. During this 'bees flight', the queen has to try to catch a single flying bee. If she succeeds, they create a new pair. The bee who has not found a new partner becomes the new queen.

(110) Standing Dance

All players stand still around the room. The leader plays some strongly rhythmic music and 'releases', one at a time, individual body parts for movement: for example, first the forehead, then the eyes, the little finger of the left hand, the mouth, the thumb of the right hand, the left hip and so on.

All movements have to be continued, even when new ones are added.

After a while, movements can, on instruction from the leader, be 'frozen' again, one by one.

(111) Fully Automatic Jointed Doll

Players are seated in a circle. One player begins by saying, 'I have a fully automatic jointed doll that does this'. The player now demonstrates a body movement – for example, stamping on the floor with their left foot. All other players copy this movement. The left-hand neighbour of the first player continues: 'I also have a fully automatic jointed doll that does this'. They demonstrate another movement, for example, opening and closing their mouth. Everybody else also has to copy this movement, but without stopping the first one. The more players that have had a turn, the more complicated it becomes to carry out all movements simultaneously. The game can be interrupted if a player says: 'My fully automatic jointed doll is broken'. Then all players have to freeze in mid-movement. Alternatively, you could agree to use those words to end the game, when no one is prepared to bring the fully automatic jointed doll back to life again.

(112) Peas Roll

The group is seated in a circle. Initially, all players practise the text in a chorus: 'Peas are rolling across the street, and then they get squashed. Oh, what a shame, what a crying, crying shame.' At the second rehearsal, corresponding movements are practised. The leader demonstrates:

◆ At 'Peas are rolling across the street, and then they get…', everybody has to walk their index and middle fingers along their upper thighs to their knees;
◆ At '…squashed…', they slap their knees with both hands;
◆ At '…Oh…', they put their left hands flat over their mouths;
◆ At '…what a shame…', they touch the side of their heads with their right hands,
◆ At '…crying, crying…', they tap their mouths twice with their left hands; and
◆ At '…shame', they put their right hands to the side of their heads again.

During the course of the game, additional instructions can be given with regard to mime, volume and tempo. For example, the peas could roll across the street laughing, crying, happily, loudly, sadly, fast, slowly, and so on. The more the instructions that have to be followed, and the faster the game is played, the greater the attention that has to be paid.

(113) Lion Hunt

All players are seated in a circle, with plenty of room to move. They mimic steps by stamping their feet and, at the same time, slap their hands on their upper thighs. During this movement, the leader begins to talk:

Leader:	Are we going on a lion hunt?
Everybody:	Yes, we are going on a lion hunt.
Leader:	Hold on, what is this? (Points with his finger.)
Everybody:	Hold on, what is that?
Leader:	Is it a lion?
Everybody:	Is it a lion?
Leader:	No, that's not a lion. (Shakes his head.)
Everybody:	No, that's not a lion.

This speech and counter-speech is the chorus. It is repeated after every stop of the journey!

Stop 1
Leader: This is a gate, we have to get through it. (Pretends to open a squeaky gate.)

Chorus

Stop 2
Leader: This is a meadow, we have to get across it. (Rubs hands together, splashes, as if wading through water.)

Chorus

Stop 3

Leader: This is a bridge, we have to get across. (Makes a sound as if crossing a wooden bridge.)

Chorus

Stop 4

Leader: This is a river, we have to get across it. (Takes his shoes off and holds them in one hand, while making swimming movements with the other.)

Chorus

Stop 5

Leader: This is a tree, we have to get across it. (Pretends to climb a tree.)

Chorus

Stop 6

Leader: This is a cave, we have to get in. (Pretends to crawl into a cave.)

This time, the chorus is not repeated, but the leader waves until it is really quiet. All of a sudden, the leader shouts: 'Hang on, what is this? – Ah, a lion!'

Now, all stations are gone through again in reverse, with the leader going through the instructions as quickly as possible. In the end, the leader says, 'There is a gate, we have to get through it.' (The squeaking of the gate is imitated.) 'The gate is closed.' (Loud bang.) And now everybody shouts a relieved 'Aah!'

114 Jungle Expedition

This game can be played in any room, as long as it is not too small. The leader slowly reads the following story, and players try to make movements corresponding to what is happening in the story. To make the image of a jungle expedition even more realistic, appropriate music can be played quietly in the background. The leader begins:

'Imagine you are on an expedition into the jungle. You are in the deepest jungle … Everything is overgrown … You cannot make out a path … Lianas hanging from the trees brush against your face … It is dark and damp … You really have to strain your eyes … You are sweating … With a lot of effort, you are clearing a way … You are using a bush knife to cut a lane … Suddenly, there is a big tree across your path … You try to climb over it … You slip … You try again … You try to swing across the tree on a liana … On the other side of the tree trunk you land in a swamp … You wade through the swamp … The mosquitoes are really bothering you … You try to fight them off … You have to protect your head from falling coconuts … You are so sweaty … You fan yourself with a big leaf … A parrot gives you a fright … You are really hungry and you pick a berry … You put it in your mouth … and spit it out again quickly … because it tastes very bitter … You are thirsting for water … You swallow … The path becomes narrower and narrower … Breathing is becoming more and more difficult ... You fall to the ground with exhaustion ... Although you fight against it, you cannot stand up anymore ... You are so tired ... Finally, you fall asleep ...'

The story can finish here. Alternatively, it can release members of the jungle expedition from their state of exhaustion and lead them to a village. The story can be embellished as much as you like, or it can become a totally different story. The only important thing is that group members are able to express the story through mime.

115 Station

The leader reads out or tells a story for which group members – at his signal – have to add voices or noises according to their roles, which have been agreed before the beginning of the game. For example, the following roles, words and sounds could be allocated:

Station master: 'Stand back, please'
Ice-cream vendor: 'Lemon ice-cream, chocolate ice-cream'
Hot dog vendor: 'Hot dogs'
Father Miller: 'Goodbye'
Lisa Miller: 'Take care'
Aunty Dot: 'Sob sob'
Uncle Henry: 'Look after yourself'
Station clock: 'Tick-tock, tick-tock'
Locomotive: 'Pfff' (loud whistle tone)
Train: 'Tschoo tschoo tschoo'
Carriage door: 'Bang'

And so on. There have to be as many roles as there are group members. With large groups, the same roles can be assigned several times. Then, the leader begins his station story:

'The hand on the station clock … is moving around. Aunty Dot … is saying goodbye to Lisa Miller … and father Miller …The station master … lifts his signalling disc, the locomotive … jerks, the carriage door … slams shut. The train … is beginning to move.

'In the background you can hear the ice-cream vendor … and the hot dog vendor … Uncle Henry calls out … Aunty Dot is crying quietly … The train … disappears into the distance. In the silence, the only thing that can be heard is the station clock.'

Again, the story can be expanded, lengthened, or totally changed in any way you like. What is important is that every group member is able to take turns – preferably with equal frequency.

116 Atte Katte Nuwa

Players sit in a circle. As an introduction, the leader briefly tells a story about an Inuit family that is going to hunt whales or seals. Afterwards, everybody learns the text and melody of the 'fishing song', so that they can go hunting with the family. While the group is singing the same text for all five verses, the leader gives instructions as to what to do. The leader always gives the first command at the beginning of the song, during the words, 'Atte katte …' (A); the second command with the words, 'Hexa …' (B); and the third one at the repetition of the words, 'Atte katte … misa de' (C). What follows are the leader's instructions, with the corresponding movements for the five song repetitions.

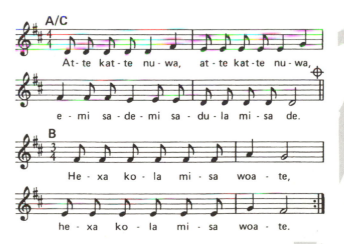

and again from the beginning until ⊕

1 A: See if you can spot a seal's (whale's) tail? (Looking in different directions with one hand above the eyes.)

B: Further out to sea! (Making paddling movements.)

C: Keep a look out! (Looking around, as A.)

2 A: Further out to sea! (Making paddling movements.)

B: Wave over the others! (Waving.)

C: And further out to sea! (Making paddling movements.)

3 A: Pass the rope! (Unrolling a rope from one arm.)

B: Ready for the catch! (Throwing the line like a lasso.)

C: We need more ropes! (Unrolling rope, as in A.)

4 A: Pull in the catch! (Slowly pulling up the rope.)

B: Lift it on board! (Effortfully heaving up the catch.)

C: Pull up more rope! (Quickly pulling up rope.)

5 A: Now pass us the bottle! (Fetching and opening a bottle.)

B: Let's drink to the catch! (Cheering.)

C: Handkerchief! (Wiping off sweat.)

Depending on the imagination of the leader, further commands and movements can be built into the story.

(**117**) On the River We Want to Go

Players are seated or stand in a circle. Making up a tune, the players sing the following words:

> On the river we want to go
> Where the boats are turning
> And one boat is called … (name of a player)
> And … (name as above) has to go.

And then the actual game begins. Everybody starts to sing. One player walks about in the middle of the circle, and incorporates any player's name into the song. The named player has to stand up and link arms with the first player. They walk around together. Now the song starts again. The last player always determines who is going to be collected next.

Players continue to sing until all players have linked up as boats and are travelling on the river.

118 An Elephant Wanted to Go for a Stroll

(A dancing song from North America)

Ein E - le - fant wollt bum - meln gehn,
sich die wei - te Welt be - sehn.

1 An elephant wants to go for a stroll
   to see the whole wide world.

2 Slowly he puts one foot in front of the other,
   because he is no bus.

3 Soon, he is not on his own any more,
   everyone tramples along behind.

4 And already the whole country is singing
   this song about the elephant.

From *Der Zuendschluessel*, Fidula Verlag, Boppard/Rhein.

The group is seated in a circle. The player who is going to play the elephant first goes and stands in the middle, then begins to trot around with big elephant steps, and this is how they go: left, right, left – three steps forward, then, on the spot, the right foot across the left one and back again, the left foot across the right one, and then the whole thing starts again from the beginning: three steps forward, starting with the left foot, and so on.

The group accompanies the 'elephant walk' by repeatedly singing the elephant song, and one player after the other links up with the 'elephants' in the middle of the circle, so that, finally, a long caravan is on its way, marching like elephants.

119 A Little Sailor

A little sailor sailed around the world. He loved a girl who had no money. The girl had to die and whose fault was that? That of a little sailor who was madly in love.

Ein klei - ner Ma - tro - se um - se - gel - te die
Welt. Er lieb - te ein Mäd - chen, das
hat - te gar kein Geld. Das Mäd - chen muß - te
ster - ben, und wer war schuld dar - an? Ein
klei - ner Ma - tro - se in sei - nem Lie - bes - wahn.

Once the melody has been practised together, the leader introduces the words with accompanying movements:

A:	indicating one with the left thumb
little:	left thumb and index finger indicate a short distance
sailor:	the left hand is put to the front of the head to salute

sailed around:	moving the fingers of both hands like waves
the world:	indicating a big circle using both hands
He loved:	hugging oneself
a:	again indicating one with the left thumb
girl:	using both hands to draw the shape of a girl's body
who had no:	shaking head
money:	counting money with two fingers
The girl:	again indicating the shape of a girl's body with both hands
had to die:	indicating cutting throat
and whose fault was that?:	drawing a question mark into the air
That of a:	indicating one with the left thumb
small:	indicating a short distance again with left thumb and index finger
sailor:	again, raising one hand to salute
who was madly in love:	again hugging oneself, and then tapping one's forehead

Now the song is sung with all the movements. Gradually, some of the words are omitted and replaced with the corresponding movements only, until, eventually, the whole song is sung 'silently'.

120 Em Pompi

(A song from Germany)

Em pom - pi pol - le - mi pol - le - mis - co
em pom - pi, em pom - pa, des - co - de - mo, keh - re
wie - der, em pom - pi und em pom - pa, o
des - co - de - mo, keh - re wie - der
in die Hei - mat - stadt zu - rück, viel Glück.

Em pompi polemi polemisco
em pompi, empompa, desco demo, return
again, em pompi and empompa, o
desco demo, return again
to your home town, good luck.

(From *Die Zugabe*, vol 3, Fidula Verlag, Boppard/Rhein.)

The group divides into pairs. Partners stand facing each other, and start clapping at every eighth note, according to the following pattern:

◆ Clapping their own hands

◆ Right hand to partner's right hand

◆ Own hands

◆ Left hand to partner's left hand

◆ Own hands

◆ Both hands to partner's hands

◆ With crossed-over hands on to own chest

◆ With both hands on to own thighs

With an uneven number of players, one player can also clap on a table instead of a partner's hands and, of course, other or additional movements – depending on imagination and fun in the game – are also possible. Begin slowly, and speed up the tempo when repeating the song.

121 A Small Grey Donkey

Ein klei-nes, grau-es E-sel-chen, das trap-pelt durch die Welt. Es wak-kelt mit dem Hin-ter-teil so, wie es ihm ge-fällt, i-a, i-a, i-a, i-a.

All players are seated on chairs in a circle, with sufficient space to be able to move around. The leader initially demonstrates the melody and words. After that, the following movements are added:

While the first part is sung everybody stays on their chairs and tramples with their feet.

In part 2, everybody stands up and wiggles their bottoms, as described in the words at the top of page 147.

In part 3, all players sit down again and nod their heads.

A small grey donkey that
tramples through the world. It wiggles with its
bottom just as it feels like,
eeyore, eeyore, eeyore, eeyore.

As soon as the group has mastered melody, words and
movements, it can be split into three sub-groups of equal size,
and the whole song can be sung as a canon! The next group
always starts at the beginning of a new part.

The group can also be split into three sub-groups right from
the beginning, the sub-groups forming circles, which rotate in
opposite directions while players sing. Alternatively, they
move around the world as wavy lines. Canons can also be
sung during these variations.

(122) Henry Nosen's Bicycle

Players are seated in a circle and sing the following words to the tune of 'Glory, glory, hallelujah':

> Henry Nosen's bicycle has a flat tyre
> Henry Nosen's bicycle has a flat tyre
> Henry Nosen's bicycle has a flat tyre
> But with chewing gum we'll fix it again!

At the same time, the following movements are made:

Henry:	pointing to oneself
Nosen's:	touching one's nose
bicycle:	indicating a circle with both hands
flat:	hissing sound or clapping hands
tyre:	covering ears with both hands, or throwing both hands up in the air
chewing gum:	miming pulling out chewing gum from one's mouth
fix it again:	indicating fixing the tyre by hand

As the game proceeds, some of the words and then some more are omitted and replaced by the corresponding movement. In the end, the song consists only of movements. Whoever wants to can gradually add in words again, until, in the end, the song is complete once more.

(123) Head and Shoulders

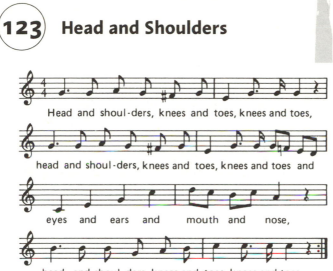

Head and shoul-ders, knees and toes, knees and toes,

head and shoul-ders, knees and toes, knees and toes and

eyes and ears and mouth and nose,

head and shoul-ders, knees and toes, knees and toes.

The group is seated in a circle. The leader initially speaks the words, and players repeat them and practise touching the body parts that feature in the text, using their fingers or hands.

Head, shoulders, knees and toes, knees and toes,
head, shoulders, knees and toes, knees and toes
and eyes and ears and mouth and nose,
head, shoulders, knees and toes, knees and toes.

Afterwards, the melody is added. Players begin slowly, gradually singing and moving faster and faster.

124 I Know a Cowboy

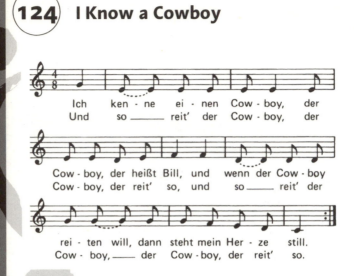

Ich ken - ne ei - nen Cow - boy, der
Und so ＿ reit' der Cow - boy, der

Cow - boy, der heißt Bill, und wenn der Cow - boy
Cow - boy, der reit' so, und so ＿ reit' der

rei - ten will, dann steht mein Her - ze still.
Cow - boy, ＿ der Cow - boy, der reit' so.

The group is seated in a circle. The leader initially sings the first part of the song: 'I know a cowboy, a cowboy, his name is Bill.' Next, the leader asks the group members to sing with him the second part of each verse, and accompany it with corresponding movements.

1   … and when the cowboy wants to ride, my little heart just stops. And this is how the cowboy rides, the cowboy rides like this, and this is how the cowboy rides, the cowboy rides like this.

2   … and when the cowboy wants to shoot …
    … and this is how the cowboy shoots …

3   … and when the cowboy throws the lasso
    … and this is how the lasso flies …

4 … and when the cowboy wants to drink
   … and this is how the cowboy drinks …
5 … and when the cowboy wants to eat …
   … and this is how the cowboy eats …
6 … and when the cowboy wants to sleep …
   … and this is how the cowboy sleeps …

Additional verses can be added, according to the mood and enthusiasm of the players. As a variation, all actions that have already been carried out can be sung after the song's beginning: 'I know a cowboy, a cowboy, his name is Bill', before a new action is added. Of course, this requires a lot more concentration.

125 I Have an Aunty

Groups that are not that enthusiastic about cowboys and the wild west may sing the following words to the tune of 'I know a cowboy' (pages 150–1):

> I have an aunty, an aunty, an aunty, who is like this
> and when aunty goes dancing,
> her little skirt goes like this.
> And like this goes her little skirt, her little skirt
> it goes like this,
> And like this goes her little skirt, her little skirt
> it goes like this.

At 'this', the movement of a swinging little skirt is indicated. The 'little skirt' can be replaced in further verses by, for example, 'little legs', 'little head', 'little arms', 'little hands', 'little feet', and so on, with the corresponding body parts being moved.

(126) If You're Happy and You Know it

1. If you're hap-py and you know it, clap your
hands. If you're hap-py and you
know it, clap your hands. If you're
hap-py and you know it and you real-ly
want to show it, if you're hap-py and you
know it, clap your hands. If you're

The leader introduces the melody and the words, and claps hands at the quarter beats marked with 'x'. In all further verses, the verse essentially stays the same – only the activity is replaced with a new one.

1 If you're happy and you know it, clap your hands.
If you're happy and you know it, clap your hands.
If you're happy and you know it and you really want to show it,
if you're happy and you know it, clap your hands.

2 … slap your sides …
3 … stamp your feet …
4 … snap your fingers …
5 … sniff your nose ….
6 … shout 'We are'.

After all verses have been sung individually, all commands can be repeated again directly one after the other. Now players can show how much attention they have been paying:

If you're happy and you know it, clap your hands – slap your sides – stamp your feet – snap your fingers – sniff your nose – shout 'We are.' If you're happy …

(127) Labadu

Tanz im-mer La - ba - du, La - ba - du,

La - ba - du, tanz im - mer La - ba - du,

La - ba - la - ba - du. Hej!

Always dance Labadu, Labadu, Labadu, always dance Labadu, Labalabadu. Hey!

(From *Spielen – Singen – Tanzen*,
Verlag Gruppenpaedagogisher Literatur, Wehrheim.)

All players are seated in a circle. The leader asks, 'Have we ever danced Labadu before?' Everybody answers, 'No!' The leader decides: 'Then we are going to dance Labadu now!'

Everyone begins to sing and dance. The same text is always repeated, and the dancing steps also remain the same: only body posture is varied with every new round.

The Labadu step goes like this: The left foot is moved to the left one step, the right foot is closed up, and this is repeated continuously. After 'Hey!', the same steps can also be made to the right again for one round.

Before the introduction of a new body posture, the leader and the group members enter a dialogue, as outlined above. For example:

Have we ever danced Labadu arm-in-arm?
Have we ever danced Labadu with our hands on our knees?
Have we ever danced Labadu squatting down?
Have we ever danced Labadu with our hands over our ears?
Have we ever danced Labadu with our hands over our neighbour's ears?

And so on.

Players are likely to think of many more movement possibilities. The more complicated and the faster the dance, the more exhausting the game becomes. Playing Labadu not only requires great concentration on one's body, it is also good fun.

(128) La Bella Polenta

This movement game is best known in its Italian version, which is why it is used first here.

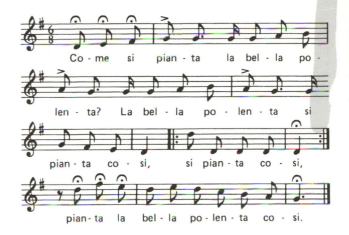

Players are seated in a circle. Everybody accompanies the singing with hand movements that fit the words of the song. In each verse, the preceding actions are repeated, so that the song becomes longer and longer.

1 Come si pianta la bella polenta? La bella polenta si pianta cosi,
   si pianta cosi, si pianta cosi, pianta la bella polenta cosi.
2 Come si cresce …?
   … si pianta cosi, si cresce cosi, cresce la bella polenta cosi.
3 Come si fiore …?
4 Come si taglia …?

5 Come si muola …?
6 Come si cuoce …?
7 Come si mangia …?
8 Come si gusta …?

(From *Der Zuendschluessel*, Fidula Verlag, Boppard/Rhein.)

The game is called 'How do we plant the nice sweetcorn?' The corresponding hand movements for verses 1–8 are as follows:

1 plant – pushing seeds into the ground
2 grow – upwards movement with hands
3 blossom – hands describe a blossom
4 cut – hands make a cutting movement
5 grind – hands move against each other to make a grinding movement
6 cook – something is stirred using hands
7 eat – a spoon is moved to the mouth
8 enjoy – rubbing the stomach

129 Laurentia

Lau - ren - tia, lie - be Lau - ren - tia mein,

wann wer - den wir wie - der zu - sam - men sein?

Am Sonn - - tag.—— Ach, wenn es doch

erst wie - der Sonn - tag wär und ich bei
Mon - tag
Diens - tag ...

mei - ner Lau - ren - tia wär, Lau - ren - tia wär!——

Laurentia, my dear Laurentia,
when are we going to be together again?
On Sunday [Monday, Tuesday …]. Oh if only it was
Sunday [Monday, Tuesday …] again
and I was with my Laurentia, with my Laurentia.

All players stand in a circle, hold hands, move to the right following the rhythm of the music, and sing the song of Laurentia. As soon as the name 'Laurentia' or a weekday is mentioned, all players do a knees-bend. In every verse, a new weekday is added, so that a further knees-bend is added, too. For example, the third verse goes like this:

Laurentia, my dear Laurentia,
when are we going to be together again?
On Tuesday.
Oh, if only it was Sunday, Monday, Tuesday again
and I was with my Laurentia, with my Laurentia.

Following this procedure, the group works its way through all
the days of the week. Older players should be warned: the
simultaneous singing, the turning around in circles and the
knees-bending at the mention of every weekday and
'Laurentia' can be very exhausting!

(130) Ma Ku Ah Koo Tee O

Ma   ku   ah   koo   tee   o   we -

i   ku   i   ta - - na   ma   ku   ah   koo

tee   o   we - i   ku   i   ta - - na.

For this game, the group divides into pairs. Each of the two partners needs two wooden sticks about 30cm long. Partners sit cross-legged opposite each other. They grip their sticks near the middle, and hold them vertically just above the floor. With the first note of the song, the following movements begin:

Ma: the sticks are struck on the floor

ku: each player's sticks are struck vertically against each other

ah: partners throw their right sticks to each other, using their right hands to catch. Be careful that the sticks do not collide in mid-air!

koo: the sticks are struck on the floor again

tee: the sticks are struck against each other vertically again

o: partners throw their left sticks to each other, using their left hands to catch.

(From Elisabeth Achtnich, *Mein Liedersack*, Burckhardthaus-Laetare Verlag GmbH, Offenbach/Main.)

From 'wei' onwards, these movements are always repeated, until the tune has finished.

Depending on the skilfulness of the players, new stick movements can be invented for further verses. The melody and the text remain the same.

(131) My Aunt from Morocco

The group is seated in a circle. The following verses are sung to the tune, 'She'll be coming round the mountain', and the exclamations at the end of the line are accompanied by hand movements. At the end of each verse, all preceding exclamations and hand movements are repeated.

1 My aunt from Morocco, when she comes, hi ho (first the left hand, then the right hand on the shoulder), my aunt from Morocco, when she comes, hi ho (movement as above), my aunt from Morocco, my aunt from Morocco, my aunt from Morocco, when she comes, hi ho (movement as above).

2 And she comes on two camels, when she comes, hopple di popp (trotting with both feet) …

3 And she'll kiss you on the cheek, when she comes, slop slop (pretend kissing in different directions) …

4 And then we drink a Coke, when she comes, slurp slurp (making drinking movements) …

5 And then we bake a cake, when she comes, knead knead (making kneading movements) …

6 And then we kill a chicken, when she comes, krr krr (making cut-throat movements) …

7 And then she writes to say, that she won't come, sob sob (making crying sounds, singing slowly) …

8 And then we eat the chicken on our own, yum yum (rubbing stomachs) …

9 And then she writes to say that she is coming after all, hooray (jumping up, arms in the air, singing faster again) …

10 And all the bells are ringing, when she comes, ding dong (bells ringing) …

After the last verse, all the noises and movements are made one more time: hi ho, hopple di popp, slop slop, slurp slurp, knead knead, krr krr, sob sob, yum yum, hooray, ding dong.

Of course, the group can invent further verses themselves.

(132) She'll be Coming Round the Mountain

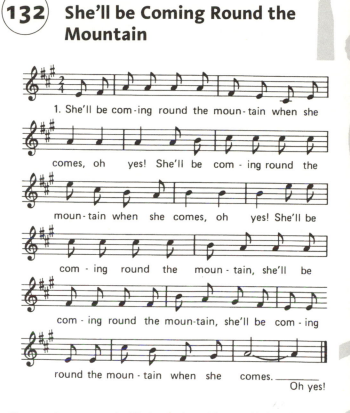

1. She'll be com-ing round the moun-tain when she comes, oh yes! She'll be com-ing round the moun-tain when she comes, oh yes! She'll be com-ing round the moun-tain, she'll be com-ing round the moun-tain, she'll be com-ing round the moun-tain when she comes. _____ Oh yes!

Every play group is likely to be able to think of suitable movements for the different verses of this English movement game:

1 She'll be coming round the mountain when she comes, oh yes!
She'll be coming round the mountain when she comes, oh yes!
She'll be coming round the mountain,

She'll be coming round the mountain,
She'll be coming round the mountain when she comes,
oh yes!

2 She'll be driving six white horses when she comes,
ho ho ...

3 Oh! we'll all go out to meet her when she comes,
hi hi ...

4 We'll kill the big old rooster when she comes,
hack hack ...

5 We'll all have chicken an' dumplings when she comes,
yum yum ...

6 She will have to sleep with grandma when she comes,
smork smork ...

7 She'll be wearing red pyjamas when she comes,
scratch scratch ...

(133) My Hat, it has Three Corners

Mein Hut, der hat drei Ek - ken, drei

Ek - ken hat mein Hut, und hat er nicht drei

Ek - ken, dann ist er nicht mein Hut.

Initially, the leader introduces the verse:

My hat, it has three corners, three corners has my hat,
and if it hasn't got three corners, it is not my hat.

The following movements are made every time the words 'my', 'hat', 'three' and 'corners' are sung:

my: everybody points to themselves
hat: making out a hat on one's head using hands
three: indicating the number with three fingers
corners: hitting the left elbow with the right hand.

During the course of the game, words are omitted gradually, and replaced by corresponding movements, so that, in the end, the song is sung 'silently'. In the same way, words can gradually be added in again, until the song is complete.

134 O Oni Goni Sad

O o - ni go - ni sad, o o - ni!

O o - ni go - ni sad, o o - ni!

Wa wa wa ha - ko da ja ja;

u - wit u - wit u - wit pi - ki - si!

The group is seated in a circle, and initially learns the words and melody. Both remain the same for each verse: only the movements change. Following the rhythm of the song, the following movements are made, verse by verse:

1 At 'O', everyone points to the middle of the circle and shapes an O, using thumb and index finger. From 'oni' onwards, everyone slaps their hand on the thigh of their left-hand neighbour, then on their own, then on that of their right-hand neighbour, and so on.

2 Everyone claps their hands twice, then slaps their own left thigh with their right hand and, after that, their right thigh with their left hand, and so on.

3 Initially, everyone forms an 'O' with their hand, and then slaps both thighs with the corresponding hands, then with hands crossed, then again with the right hand on the right thigh, and with the left hand on the left thigh, then quickly bending their arms and making an 'o', and so on.

4 The left arm is stretched out forwards, then the left hand is slapped with the right hand, touches the right arm bend and the left arm is bent. Now the same movement follows with the right arm and right hand, and so on.

5 Both hands slap the thighs, then the left hand is moved to the nose and, at the same time, the right hand is moved to the left ear. Afterwards, both hands slap the thighs again, and then the right hand touches the nose, and the left hand is moved to the right ear, and so on.

It is not that easy to carry out these movements correctly. Groups that have mastered the movements sing faster and faster, and the game becomes more and more difficult.

(135) Sitting Boogie

Players are seated in a circle. The leader initially introduces the tune, singing, 'la la la ...' Then all players carry out the following movements to the rhythm of the music:

Bar 1: Using both hands, slap the thighs twice, and clap hands twice.

Bar 2: Using short sideways movements, cross both hands twice with the back of the hands facing upwards, right hand on top. Repeat with the left hand on top.

Bar 3: Push both hands diagonally downwards to the right twice, and afterwards twice down to the left.

Bar 4: Bow to the left, and bow to the right.

At the repetition of the tune, the second series of movements begins:

Bar 5: Right lower arm points upwards in an elegant movement and is shaken out; at the same time, the left hand touches the right elbow. This is repeated the other way around.

Bar 6:   The right hand, palm pointing forward, moves the thumb to the temple and waves fingers. Repeat with the left hand.

Bar 7:   Right thigh is lifted diagonally forward, then the left.

Bar 8:   Stand up and sit down again.

And then the boogie starts again from the beginning. The more frequently the four bars are repeated, the more the tempo needs to be increased. Players sing and dance as long as they are having fun, and until they are out of breath.

136 Someone's in the Kitchen with Dinah

Some-one's in the kit-chen with Di - nah,
Tom sitzt in der Kü-che mit Ti - na,

some-one's in the kit-chen I know-o-o-o,
Tom sitzt in der Kü-che mit Ti - na - a - a,

some-one's in the kit-chen with Di - nah,
Tom sitzt in der Kü-che mit Ti - na

strum-min' on the old ban - jo._____
und er spiel-te sein Ban - jo._____

Fee - fi - fidd-le ei - o, fee-fi-fidd-le ei -
Di - di di-del di-del-dum, di - di di-del di-del-

o - o - o - o, fee - fi - fidd-le ei-o,
dum,_____ di - di di-del dei-dum,

strum-min' on the old ban - jo._____
und er spiel-te sein Ban - jo._____

Someone's in the kitchen with Dinah
someone's in the kitchen, I know, o o o
someone's in the kitchen with Dinah
strumming on the old banjo.
Fee fi fiddle ei o, fee fi fiddle ei o o o o,
fee fi fiddle ei o, strumming on the old banjo.

While singing the individual verses, players pretend to play invisible instruments.

1 Someone's in the kitchen with Dinah …
strumming on the old banjo.
Fee fi fiddle ei o
strumming on the old banjo.
2 … on the old piano
3 … on the old trumpet
4 … on the old guitar
5 … on the old bass
6 … on the old drums

Anyone who wants to can add further instruments. The game can also be played with an additional movement: everybody claps their hands simultaneously, then claps hands with their neighbour on their left; on their own again, and then with their neighbour on the right, and so on.

137 What Sort of Trees Must they be?

Was müs-sen das für Bäu-me sein,

wo die gro-ßen E-le-fan-ten spa-

zie-ren gehn, oh-ne sich zu sto-ßen!

Rechts sind Bäu-me, links sind Bäu-me,

und da-zwi-schen Zwi-schen-räu-me,

wo die gro-ßen E-le-fan-ten spa-

zie-ren gehn, oh-ne sich zu sto-ßen.

What sort of trees must they be, where the big elephants go for a walk without bumping into anything?